Hemingway
and Film

UNGAR FILM LIBRARY
Stanley Hochman
General Editor

Academy Awards: An Ungar Reference Index, *edited by Richard Shale*

American History / American Film: Interpreting the Hollywood Image, *edited by John O'Connor and Martin A. Jackson*

The Classic American Novel and the Movies, *edited by Gerald Peary and Roger Shatzkin*

The Blue Angel / *the novel by Heinrich Mann and the film by Josef von Sternberg*

Costume Design in the Movies / *Elizabeth Leese*

Faulkner and Film / *Bruce F. Kawin*

Fellini the Artist / *Edward Murray*

Film Study Collections: A Guide to their Development and Use / *Nancy Allen*

Hitchcock / *Eric Rohmer and Claude Chabrol*

Loser Take All: The Comic Art of Woody Allen / *Maurice Yacowar*

The Modern American Novel and the Movies, *edited by Gerald Peary and Roger Shatzkin*

On the Verge of Revolt: Women in American Films of the Fifties / *Brandon French*

Ten Film Classics / *Edward Murray*

Tennessee Williams and Film / *Maurice Yacowar*

OTHER FILM BOOKS

The Age of the American Novel: The Film Aesthetic of Fiction between the Two Wars / *Claude-Edmonde Magny*

The Cinematic Imagination: Writers and the Motion Pictures / *Edward Murray*

A Library of Film Criticism: American Film Directors, *edited by Stanley Hochman*

Nine American Film Critics / *Edward Murray*

HEMINGWAY AND FILM

Gene D. Phillips

FREDERICK UNGAR PUBLISHING CO.
New York

Copyright © 1980 by Frederick Ungar Publishing Co., Inc.
Printed in the United States of America
Designed by H. Roberts

Library of Congress Cataloging in Publication Data

Phillips, Gene D
    Hemingway and film.

    Bibliography: p.
    Includes index.
    1. Hemingway, Ernest, 1899–1961—Film adaptations.
2. Film adaptations. I. Title.
PS3515.E37Z754   813'.52   80–7563
ISBN 0-8044-2695-3
ISBN 0-8044-6644-0 (pbk.)

To Henry King

All stories, if continued far enough, end in death; and he is no true storyteller who would keep that from you. . . . If two people love each other there can be no happy end to it.

—Ernest Hemingway
Death in the Afternoon

Contents

Acknowledgments

Fɪʀsᴛ ᴏꜰ ᴀʟʟ ɪ ᴀᴍ ᴍᴏsᴛ ɢʀᴀᴛᴇꜰᴜʟ ᴛᴏ
Mary Hemingway, who corresponded with me about the film versions of Ernest Hemingway's fiction and encouraged me in this project.

I would also like to single out the following people among those who gave me their help:

Henry King, who directed *The Snows of Kilimanjaro* and *The Sun Also Rises*, for giving me a lengthy interview especially for this book.

Fred Zinnemann, who answered my questions about his work on *The Old Man and the Sea*, part of which he directed; film directors Howard Hawks, Don Siegel, and Franklin Schaffner, and cinematographer James Wong Howe, all of whom talked with me when they appeared at the Chicago Film Festival during the years that I was doing remote preparation on this study, and all of whom have been involved in Hemingway films.

Bruce Kawin, author of the introductory essay for the

published film script of *To Have and Have Not*, for allowing me to read his essay before it appeared in print, as well as Tino Balio, general editor of the University of Wisconsin Press film script series, publisher of the essay and the script.

Film scholar Lester Keyser for making available to me the final shooting scripts of several of the Hemingway films.

Alfred Gini, my colleague at Loyola University, for giving me a tour of the house in which Hemingway grew up and of other points of interest in Oak Park, Illinois, associated with the young Hemingway, during the time in which Mr. Gini lived in the Hemingway home.

Patrick Sheehan of the Motion Picture Section of the Library of Congress in Washington, D.C.; Mary Corliss of the Film Stills Archive of the Museum of Modern Art in New York City; Stuart Kaminsky of the Film Department of Northwestern University in Chicago and screenwriter Alan Wilson for providing me with research materials; film scholar Leo Murray for his valuable suggestions; and Mary Ellen Hayes for coordinating the filmography.

Loyola University for granting me an academic leave in order to complete this project, as well as the Research Committee of Loyola University for giving me a summer grant for the same purpose.

The New York Times Book Review for publishing my query for data about Hemingway and the films of his fiction, which brought me some information that I would not have otherwise known about.

Acknowledgment is made also for the use of Carlos Baker's essay on Ernest Hemingway, which appears as the foreword to this book; it is reprinted with permission of *Saturday Review* in which it originally appeared and is copyrighted by *Saturday Review*, 1961. All rights reserved.

Chronology

1928 Moves to Key West, Florida. Dr. Hemingway commits suicide.

1929 Publication of *A Farewell to Arms*, a novel.

1932 Publication of *Death in the Afternoon*, a study of bullfighting. Release of the first Hemingway screen adaptation, *A Farewell to Arms*.

1933 Publication of *Winner Take Nothing*, another short story collection.

1935 Publication of *The Green Hills of Africa*, a study of big game hunting.

1937 Publication of *To Have and Have Not*, a novel. Collaborates on a documentary about the Spanish Civil War called *The Spanish Earth* while serving as correspondent for the North American Newspaper Alliance in Spain.

1938 Publication of *The Fifth Column*, a play, as part of a book that also includes "The Snows of Kilimanjaro" and "The Short Happy Life of Francis Macomber."

1940 *The Fifth Column*, revised by Benjamin Glazer, has a brief Broadway run. Publication of *For Whom the Bell Tolls*, a novel. Divorces Pauline Pfeiffer Hemingway to marry Martha Gellhorn and settles at Finca Vigía (Lookout Farm) in Cuba.

1942 Serves as a war correspondent for *Collier's* in Europe, and stays on until nearly the end of the war.

1943 Release of the film version of *For Whom the Bell Tolls*.

1944 Participates in the Normandy landing on D-Day and in the liberation of Paris. Release of the film of *To Have and Have Not*.

1946 Marries Mary Welsh after divorcing Martha Gellhorn Hemingway. Release of the first film version of *The Killers*.

1947 Release of the film *The Macomber Affair*, based on "The Short Happy Life of Francis Macomber."

1950 Publication of *Across the River and into the Trees*, a novel. Release of the film version of "My Old Man" entitled

Under My Skin and of the remake of *To Have and Have Not* called *The Breaking Point*.

1952 Publication of *The Old Man and the Sea*, a novella. Release of the film version of *The Snows of Kilimanjaro*.

1953 Awarded the Pulitzer Prize for *The Old Man and the Sea*. Suffers two airplane crashes while on a safari in Africa and is reported dead by the world press.

1954 Wins the Nobel Prize for Literature.

1957 Release of the film version of *The Sun Also Rises* and of the remake of *A Farewell to Arms*.

1958 Release of another remake of *To Have and Have Not*, this time entitled *The Gun Runners*, and of the movie version of *The Old Man and the Sea*.

1961 After moving to Ketchum, Idaho, in the wake of the Castro revolution, commits suicide on July 2.

1962 Release of the film based on the Nick Adams stories, *Hemingway's Adventures of a Young Man*.

1964 Posthumous publication of *A Moveable Feast*, a memoir of his Paris days. Release of the remake of *The Killers*.

1972 Posthumous publication of *Islands in the Stream*, a novel.

1977 Release of the screen adaptation of *Islands in the Stream*.

1977 Television version of *My Old Man* first telecast December 7 in a two-hour adaptation.

Hemingway's Lasting Appeal
by Carlos Baker

LIKE THE SOUND OF THE EMBATTLED farmers' muskets at Lexington long ago, the report of the shotgun in the morning quiet of the house in Idaho went echoing across the airways to every corner of the world. Once more, as had happened after the airplane crashes seven years before in Africa, obituary notices darkly spelled it out on all the front pages in all the languages around the globe. He had read the first ones, in those days, with ironic amusement. These he could not see. In a hundred shapes and sizes, fortune had tried him before. Always before he had managed to survive. Now, unbelievably, the embattled old lion was dead. . . .

Despite certain shortcomings to which we shall shortly come, the literary historians are perfectly correct in their view that Hemingway's arrival in the middle Twenties began a new epoch in American fiction. That lucid prose which struck us so squarely a full generation ago, the famous style with its special quality of seething emotional force held in check by an iron will, that aura of romantic glamour with which the young author managed to invest the lives, loves, and locales of his earlier protagonists—these have retained their power to hold and move us as they did in that far-off world between the wars when Hemingway rose with such rapidity from apprenticeship to mastery. Nor is the secret of his continuing success difficult to explain. He kept his eyes open, all his other senses alert, his subjects limited but whole, his objects in sharp focus, and his themes as universal as courage, love, honor, endurance, suffering, death and their antonymous equivalents. Other masters, other modes—and the more the merrier. But for any who seek counsel as to how a writer can guarantee the survival of what he has written, Hemingway's esthetic prescription is unassailable.

Around the hard core of his central achievement, certain marginal limitations were early apparent. His native medium was prose fiction, and on those occasions when he stepped gingerly and experimentally into other genres, the results were seldom happy.

However deeply one sympathized in 1939 with the cause of the defeated Spanish Loyalists, *The Fifth Column* did not then play—nor does it now read—like the work of an experienced playwright. For Hemingway's was not, in any sense that matters, a theatrical mind. What Yeats scornfully called "theater business, management of men" in no way moved or attracted him. Except for the film version of *For Whom the Bell Tolls*, ably acted by his good friends Gary Cooper and Ingrid Bergman, and his friend Spencer Tracy's creation of the role of Santiago in *The Old Man and the Sea*, Hemingway could hardly endure to sit through the cinematic or the televised versions of any of his works. Like his own personal arrivals and departures, the stories made "good copy." But their true inward significance, that subtle quality which was Hemingway's genuine, personalized imprimatur, never quite survived translation, unless momentarily, from printed to dramatized versions. This is not unusual. Literary classics as various as *The Scarlet Letter*, *Great Expectations*, *War and Peace*, and *Moby Dick* have suffered similar diminutions. That unique and always delicate rapport which occurs between a great fiction writer in his privacy and the absorbed reader in his own must be distorted and is frequently destroyed.

In his other experiments with non-fiction Hemingway sometimes alienated those who did not share his over-evident passions for hunting and bullfighting. Edmund Wilson, for example, was put off by the master's ruthless self-portrait in *Green Hills of Africa*, and even professedly bored by the teeming wildlife of Tanganyika. Though *The Sun Also Rises* long ago converted a considerable segment of the American college population to the febrile joys of the annual *corridas* at Pamplona, many readers remain cool to the charms of *tauromaquia* as well as to the pontifical tone that booms through the instructional pages of *Death in the Afternoon*. For any to whom the central subject of that book is of little moment, there are always the incidental rewards to be gained from the sidelong insights that the book provides into Hemingway's most characteristic ideas, attitudes, and critical opinions.

We come finally to the fiction, both short and long, by which Hemingway's posthumous reputation must stand firm or, as is unlikely, gradually disintegrate. There is already wide agreement that his weakest work may be found in *To Have and Have Not* and *Across the River and Into the Trees*. Yet it is essential that these books should be seen against the full panorama of his other works, and that their respective virtues should not be allowed to dissolve in a generalized cloud of contumely. In the first book the three good tough monolithic stories about Harry Morgan, the desperate and laconic privateer, would have made an excellent three-part short story if Hemingway had been content to confine himself to Morgan instead of trying to unify the shorter pieces through the agency of the contrasting and much inferior story of Richard Gordon, the sold-out writer. With *Across the River* the problems were different. He had been more profoundly disturbed by the horrors of the Second World War than he publicly admitted. Death by infection had recently stared him in the face. Another marriage had gone by the board, and at fifty he could show only three major novels and the collected short stories for a quarter-century of labor. His attempt to fashion a winter's lyric of love and death in Venice did not wholly succeed. Once again he should have been willing to settle for a shorter book than he finally produced. But *Across the River* is much better, for all its shortcomings, than is now generally conceded. Time will indemnify its virtues. Let any who doubt this try rereading it now that the author is dead.

Two years after *Across the River* came *The Old Man and the Sea* to reveal once again the awesome lyrical power that Hemingway could still command so long as he remained content with a limited action and a shorter form. Those who looked back over his career from the vantage point of 1952 were struck by the fact that he had produced no full-length fiction since *For Whom the Bell Tolls* in 1940. Even when we remember that a long and exhausting war had intervened, in which Hemingway was a full participant, it was beginning to be clear as early as nine years before that the master was starting to slow down. Subsequent bad luck did not help. The severe injuries he sustained in the African plane crashes and the ill health of several subsequent years explain why—with the exceptions above noted—his reputation as a writer must now rest on five volumes: the superb short stories, *The Old Man and the Sea* and that trio of indubitable masterpieces, *The Sun Also Rises, A Farewell to Arms,* and *For Whom the Bell Tolls.* If we pause to reflect that all of these but the Santiago story were done before 1941, there are grounds for sadness, surely, though the fact is not necessarily more tragic than the ordinary course of life itself. One is grateful for such high quality wherever and whenever it appears. If we are lucky enough to have still more in this posthumous period, let it come. If not, let it go. Hemingway's best was very good indeed.

1
Take the Money and Run: Hemingway and Hollywood

Ernest Hemingway once said that the best way for a writer to deal with Hollywood was to arrange a rendezvous with the movie men at the California state line: "you throw them your book, they throw you the money, then you jump into your car and drive like hell back the way you came."[1] This is Hemingway's customarily laconic way of saying that to a novelist the film versions of his work offer a source of revenue but little else.

Furthermore Hemingway steadfastly refused to work on the screenplays of his fiction because he felt that when a writer went to Hollywood he had to write "as though you were looking through a camera lens. All you think about is pictures, when you ought to be thinking about people."[2] He broke his resolution about collaborating on a film only once, in the case of *The Old Man and the Sea*, and afterward very much regretted doing so. Hemingway's abiding personal dissatisfaction with the films of his fiction, mentioned by Carlos Baker in the preceding essay, testifies to the gulf that separates one artistic medium from another—even though in general cinema has more in common with fiction than with any other literary form.

One might be tempted to suppose that drama is closer to film than fiction is, since a play, like a movie, is acted out. But there the similarity really ends. For both a novel and a film depend more on description and narration than on dialogue, while in a play the emphasis is reversed. Novelist Robert Nathan, in affirming the closeness of fiction and film, calls a movie "a novel to be seen instead of told." The motion picture, like the novel, "ranges where it pleases; it studies the reactions of single characters; it deals in description and mood; it follows, by means of the camera, the single, unique vision of the writer. You will find, in every novel, the counterparts of long shots and close-ups, trucking shots, and dissolves; but you will find them in words addressed to the ear, instead of pictures meant for the eye."[3]

Nevertheless, in emphasizing the close relationship that undoubtedly exists between fiction and film, one must not forget that they still remain two different media of expression. Hence inevitable differences arise between the way that a story can be presented in a novel and on the screen. Compression becomes an important factor in making a motion picture from a novel, since the novelist can take as many pages as he likes to develop his plot and characters, whereas the scriptwriter has only a couple of hours of screen time at most.

One way for the screenwriter to handle this problem is to select what he considers to be the key sections of his literary source and to develop them in his script to their full dramatic potential, rather than to try to present, survey-fashion, all of the events in the original narrative material. For example, screenwriter Aaron E. Hotchner compressed Hemingway's series of Nick Adams stories into a screenplay of manageable length for filming called *Hemingway's Adventures of a Young Man* by choosing ten of the stories which constituted for him the key episodes which he wanted to dramatize in the movie.

Then he devised expository scenes which would serve as transitions from one incident to the next.

George Bluestone sums up the difficulties of adapting fiction to the screen this way in his seminal book *Novels into Film:* "Like two intersecting lines, novel and film meet at a point and then diverge. At the intersection, the book and shooting script are almost indistinguishable. But where the lines diverge, they . . . lose all resemblance to each other, for each works within the framework of its own conventions."[4] For example, it might take a novelist several phrases to build up a description of a given object, whereas the filmmaker can show the same thing on the screen in a single image.

If compression is a key factor in adapting novels like *A Farewell to Arms* and *For Whom the Bell Tolls* to the screen, expansion is a central element in bringing a short story like "The Killers" or "The Snows of Kilimanjaro" to the screen. The task confronting a screenwriter charged with creating a script from a short story is that of inventing a sufficient amount of additional material to stretch the original story into a feature-length film—without at the same time totally obliterating the point of the original story amid the intricacies of the extended story line. The tendency of a scriptwriter working on a short story is to pile on additional incidents merely to lengthen the script, instead of developing the characters and plot in greater depth to enable the viewer to gain a deeper understanding of the characters and the motivation of their behavior. It will be interesting to see in the ensuing pages how Hemingway's short fiction has fared in the hands of the Hollywood moviemakers in this regard.

Another difficulty involved in the transferral of fiction to film, whether it be long or short, is determining to what extent the original dialogue of the story can be incorporated into the screenplay. Given the naturalistic flavor of Hemingway's dialogue, it might seem that it could be just as appropriately spoken on the screen as written on the page. But, as we shall see in examining films like Selznick's *A*

Farewell to Arms, which drew heavily on Hemingway's dialogue, his dialogue is essentially literary and not dramatic. "What has the right rhythm in the book," Graham Greene has told me, "may seem unrealistic on the screen and must be modified. Dialogue in fiction must have the flavor of realism without having to be real, while on the screen the camera emphasizes the realism of the situation. You have to be closer in a film to real-life conversation in order that the dialogue will match the realistic furnishings of the sets, so to speak."

By the same token, it has often been declared by film critics and literary critics alike that Hemingway's narrative technique is cinematic, when in reality any affinity between his narrative style and filmic narration is purely superficial. It is true that much of Hemingway's narration is constructed in a straightforward fashion with vivid characters and lots of dialogue, external action, and visual detail, all of which are easily dramatized on the screen. But, as Edward Murray insists in *The Cinematic Imagination* (1972), Hemingway's work is punctuated with delicate internal monologues which mirror subjective psychological states in which a character expresses his thoughts and feelings about his experiences past or present. These interior monologues can sound very artificial and pretentious when verbalized by an actor on the sound track.

In addition, the hallmark of Hemingway's skill as a writer is his capacity to make words connote so much more than their mere literal meaning would suggest. "The things that matter to Hemingway, love, sex, death, and courage, are seldom expressed but always understood," as Peter Walsh puts it.[5] This ability to make every word count sprang, of course, from Hemingway's early apprenticeship as a newspaper reporter. He compared the allusiveness of his style to an iceberg, only one-eighth of which is visible above water. If the writer is writing truly enough, he continued, the reader will infer as much meaning from what he has written as if it had all been stated explicitly.[6]

Screenwriter Ben Hecht once described the subtle nuances of Hemingway's prose by complaining, "The son-of-a-bitch writes on water." Putting it another way, Aldous Huxley noted, "Hemingway's gift is that he writes in the white spaces between the lines." And as Murray comments on Huxley's remark, the frustration of the filmmaker trying to visualize a Hemingway work for the cinema is that "the camera cannot photograph 'the white spaces between the lines.' "[7]

Still another problem that militated against the creation of authentic film versions of Hemingway's fiction was the commercial consideration that dictated arbitrary changes calculated to bring the film versions more into line with what Hollywood producers cynically thought to be the expectations and preferences of the mass audience. Thus happy endings were manufactured for several Hemingway films simply because the studios assumed that most moviegoers would stay away from a motion picture that ended as unhappily as many of Hemingway's stories do. There is no doubt that these concessions to popular taste caused alterations in the film adaptations of Hemingway's works and that they to some degree distorted the spirit and meaning of these same works. And it is precisely the spirit and theme of the original story that must, above all else, be preserved throughout the transformation of the story from one medium to the other—regardless of the superficial changes which the plot must undergo in the process.

As film scholar Maurice Yacowar has noted, the faithful adaptation "is not one that makes no changes, but one in which the changes serve the intention and thrust of the original."[8] If the basic intent of the story has been somehow mislaid between page and screen, the original author has just grounds for complaint; and we shall shortly see that Hemingway complained a great deal about what he considered to be the unjustified liberties taken with his fiction when it was filmed.

"The matter of responsibility in adapting a fine novel is, I guess, mostly a matter of respect for the material, for what you feel the author tried to say," Jerry Wald, the producer of *Hemingway's Adventures of a Young Man* and of *The Breaking Point*, has written. "It is this, rather than any exact use of characters, dialogue, and incident, which will make it come off on the screen. . . . Only the most gifted of screenwriters can keep the intent, the flavor, the theme, and the spirit of the original."[9]

What, then, is the thematic vision that permeates the fiction of Hemingway which the moviemakers have sought with varying degrees of success to encapsulate in the films of his work? The abiding theme of Hemingway's fiction centers around the concept that in order to live a meaningful existence man must formulate a code of principles by which he judges his own behavior and thereby can achieve self-realization and fulfillment. The code which Hemingway constructed for his fictional heroes to live by can be summarized in the motto that the honorable man must live and die with courage. Furthermore, Hemingway characterized courage as "grace under pressure" because one can never be sure if he possesses the virtue of courage until it has been tested under stress.

Hemingway observed that the cult of courage was in fact age-old, and that man had always saluted this virtue by surrounding it with rituals that enhanced its practice. The ceremonies of the bullring and the military parade ground, for instance, attest to man's respect for the courage that is demonstrated in the sports arena and on the battlefield. Death-defying sports such as bullfighting and big game hunting are to be revered precisely because, like warfare, they involve the risk of death; for the proximity of death enables one to view life from a sharper perspective and with keener insight, and consequently gives one a firmer grip on reality.

The Hemingway code of courage and honor is concretized in different ways in different circumstances. Thus, the code of the warrior demands that innocent civilians be treated humanely; and the code of the hunter requires that the prey be fairly stalked and killed. Consequently, Hemingway's concepts of courage and honor do not involve a mindless, chest-pounding cult of the he-man, but a wholesome respect for playing the game of life by the rules. For those who behave dishonorably in the sporting arena will not live up to the obligations of honor and courage in other areas of life either. Hence Hemingway focuses on sportsmen and soldiers in his fiction because their struggles to vindicate their respective codes of behavior provide important metaphors for the stoic endurance which every human being must strive to possess in the face of the struggles and reversals of life from which no one is immune. All of us, at one time or another, are called upon to exhibit grace under pressure.

Hemingway's code amounts to a kind of natural religion, a spin-off from Roman Catholicism, to which Hemingway was converted under fire during World War I. "Above all other Christian beliefs," John Pratt explains, Roman Catholicism is a "code religion," with traditionally explicit rules to live by, and is "ritualistic in precisely the manner Hemingway found so appealing in aspects of war, sport, and life itself. True, his sympathetically treated Roman Catholic characters practice and believe in their religion; but they also subscribe in a more general sense to . . . the Hemingway code."[10] One readily thinks of the matador Pedro Romero in *The Sun Also Rises* and of the aged fisherman Santiago in *The Old Man and the Sea* as characters who substantiate Pratt's contention.

Hemingway's eclectic approach to religion as presented in his work also included the pantheistic notion that nature in the sublimity of its pristine, unspoiled state as one experiences it in the woods and in the mountains, brings one into the closest contact with God that is possible on this earth. The remainder of the landscape has been so smeared with the mark of man that no reflection of divinity can be discerned in it. Throughout Hemingway's writings, literary critic Scott

Donaldson observes, there runs "a lament for the past, for the days when nature had been uncontaminated by exposure to swarms of people and machinery."[11] Accordingly, contact with nature wherever it can be found in its still untainted state purifies Hemingway's heroes and refurbishes their moral stamina.

When one speaks of Hemingway's heroes one is really talking about two different varities of heroes that run through his fiction, either or both of which may appear in a given story.

Critic Philip Young distinguishes these two types as, first, a fictionalized picture of the author himself at various stages of his life and, second, the code hero, an admirable individual who lives up to his personal code of conduct in a way that serves as an inspiration for the first, the Hemingway hero. Because of the master/disciple relationship of the two types of hero in Hemingway's fiction, Arthur Waldhorn in his *Reader's Guide to Hemingway* prefers to call the Hemingway hero as described by Philip Young the apprentice hero. I too prefer this latter term and will adopt its use from this point onward, since it more clearly indicates how the disciple is learning the trade of coping with life from the code hero.

The personal names and identities of the apprentice heroes and of the code heroes may change from one Hemingway story to the next, but their relationship never does. The code hero is always the consummate professional who illustrates for the apprentice hero how his code of courage and honor is applied in practice.

The code hero is notably resilient in absorbing both the physical and psychological wounds which life inflicts on him. But the apprentice hero is not quite as impervious; though the latter's physical scars may sometimes heal, his psychic scars seldom if ever do. The apprentice hero, comments Philip Young, is "the big, tough, outdoor man," but he is also "the wounded man," an alienated figure disillusioned and disabled by the adversities of life.[12] Still, the apprentice hero struggles onward to model his behavior on that of the code hero, who serves as a kind of father figure for him.

As the apprentice hero gradually matures in book after book under the tutelage of the code hero, he steadily closes the gap between himself and the code hero. Thus Robert Jordan in *For Whom the Bell Tolls* is closer to being a code hero than is Nick Adams in Hemingway's early short stories. By the same token, the code heroes also grow in stature in the course of Hemingway's fiction, from the failed prizefighter Ole Andreson in the Nick Adams story entitled "The Killers" to Santiago in *The Old Man and the Sea*, the supreme code hero in all of Hemingway.

If Hemingway's apprentice heroes never manage to attain the full status of code heroes in his fiction, it is not because they do not try to do so. "No one of us lives by as rigid standards nor has as good ethics as we planned," Hemingway himself reflected late in life, "but an attempt is made."[13] And it is just this attempt by the apprentice heroes of Hemingway's fiction to conduct their lives according to the code of courage and honor demonstrated by the code hero which the novelist celebrates in his fiction, and which should likewise be celebrated in the film adaptations of his work.

I do not mean to suggest that in order to produce an authentic screen version of one of Hemingway's works a given screenwriter should be familiar with the recurring thematic pattern according to which the apprentice hero and the code hero appear as complementary figures in Hemingway's fiction. But I do suggest that if the scriptwriter is conscientious in his efforts to create a reasonably faithful adaptation of a Hemingway story, the code and/or apprentice heroes contained in the original story will automatically be depicted in the motion picture version in the way in which Hemingway conceived them. In the chapters to come, therefore, I shall explore the extent to which the film adaptations have succeeded in capturing the personal vision which emerges from Hemingway's fiction.

To say that a faithful rendition of a work of fiction on the screen should preserve the spirit and overall thrust of the original story is not to imply that the personal style of the film director is not important to the artistic success of a film. Richard Corliss rightly reminds us in *Talking Pictures* that "the importance of a director's personal—or even visual—style is not in question here, only the assumption that he creates a style out of thin air," instead of adapting it to the exigencies of the story which he is filming. While it is true that the director is ultimately responsible *for* the overall quality and artistic unity of a motion picture, it is also true, says Corliss, that "he must be responsible *to* something: the screenplay."[14] As writer-director Richard Brooks once remarked, "You have nothing to direct until you have a story."

The basic thrust of this book, then, is to examine the relationship of film and fiction as reflected in the screen versions of the work of one novelist, Ernest Hemingway. That this is a fruitful venture is proved by the fact that what one learns about the integration of literature and film as complementary media enhances one's appreciation of both media. As film scholar Bernard Dick has written on the relationship of fiction and film, the directors who bring the work of a great writer to the screen are really doing with images what the original author did with words: "they shape them into art."[15]

In the case of the Hemingway films, such first-class movie directors as Howard Hawks, Frank Borzage, Michael Curtiz, and Henry King have been involved in shaping Hemingway's fiction into cinematic art. And we shall see with what success they have done so.

In the last analysis, Bluestone contends, what a conscientious filmmaker is doing when he adapts a literary work to the movie medium is constructing a cinematic paraphrase of the original work. The resulting film can never be a replica of the novel or short story from which it was derived, for a work of art conceived in terms of the techniques of one medium always resists to some extent conversion into another medium; but the adapter telling the story in the new medium can, for all of that, preserve the original author's thematic intent and personal vision.

Now let me turn to the individual film adaptations of Hemingway's works. In doing so I shall briefly consider each of his stories as a work of fiction in its own right, independent of the fact that it was later to serve as the source of a screenplay. For it is only in appreciating each work in itself, as Hemingway originally conceived it, that we can properly grasp the relative merits of the film based on it.

In the end I am confident that it will become clear that despite Hemingway's feelings to the contrary, every one of these movies retains at least some moments that are true to his original work, and that at least some of them rank as examples of superior cinema, just as the novels and short stories on which they are based rank as superior fiction. After all, as Somerset Maugham once quipped, "If your characters are well conceived, they can withstand anything—even Hollywood."[16]

2
Men at War:
A Farewell to Arms
(1932 and 1957)

IT IS JUST A SHORT WALK FROM THE Victorian house where Ernest Miller Hemingway was born on July 21, 1899, at 439 North Oak Park Avenue in Oak Park, a suburb of Chicago, to the mansion which his father built at the behest of his mother at 600 North Kenilworth Avenue. A plaque in the front yard of the latter house announces that in this home Ernest Hemingway "lived in his boyhood years and created his first literary efforts." From there one can easily stroll to the nearby park where a war memorial erected in honor of those who took part in the First World War includes the name E.M. Hemingway.

These three landmarks neatly sum up Hemingway's early years. The son of Dr. Clarence and Grace Hall Hemingway, young Ernest grew restless with suburban life after high school and decided to see the world beyond Oak Park. He first did a stint as a cub reporter on the *Kansas City Star*, and then in 1918 joined the Red Cross ambulance corps (a defective eye inherited from his mother prohibited his enlisting as a soldier). He was dispatched to the Italian theater of war. "I was an awful dope when I went to the last war," he opined years later. "I remember just thinking that we were the home team and the Austrians were the visiting team."[1]

Although the teenaged Hemingway was not aware of it at the time, he was storing up experiences that he would later pour into his great novel of World War I, *A Farewell to Arms*. Not the least of these experiences was the leg wound he sustained on the night of July 8, 1918, near the village of Fossalta di Piave, where he was hit by mortar fragments and machine-gun fire. (The two citations for bravery which he received after this incident can still be seen today on display in his home in Key West.) Lt. Frederic Henry, the hero of *A Farewell to Arms*, was to be hospitalized by a war injury, as were the heroes of the Nick Adams stories and of *The Sun Also Rises*. Philip Young is quite right in contending that in each case this physical wound is meant both to symbolize and to sum up the psychic wounds which the apprentice hero suffers in the course of his life.

Several of the people whom Hemingway met while in Italy were to serve as the real-life counterparts of characters in the novel, which made use of his war experiences. For example, Don Giuseppi Bianchi, the young Italian chaplain from the Abruzzi who received Hemingway into the Catholic Church while he was awaiting surgery in a makeshift field hospital, was to find his way into the novel, as was Ernest's friend Capt. Enrico Serena, who would become Frederic Henry's sidekick, Capt. Rinaldi. But most important, the British nurse with whom Frederic falls in love was to be modeled on an American nurse in her late twenties named Agnes von Kurowsky with whom the much younger Hemingway fell desperately in love while recuperating in a Milan military hospital.

Agnes's polite but firm refusal of his marriage proposal all but shattered the young Hemingway; and there is no doubt that the grand passion between Frederic and Catherine that serves as the center of *Farewell* was something of a belated wish fulfillment for the love affair that the author never consummated with Agnes. Hemingway was to write several short stories and *The Sun Also Rises* before he felt mature enough both as a person and as a writer to deal in his fiction with his experiences of love and war with any degree of depth. He initially laid out the plot of *A Farewell to Arms* as a short story, but eventually decided that his plot and theme required a more ambitious work.

Hemingway decided to frame the story in first-person narration in order to involve the reader in the book more immediately. Frederic's personal account of how he loved and lost Catherine Barkley makes clear that he has matured as a human being because of his relationship with the selfless and devoted Catherine. Nevertheless, Catherine as Hemingway paints her seems almost too good to be true, so self-effacing is she in her single-minded commitment to Frederic. After reading the book, F. Scott Fitzgerald told Hemingway that the latter was seeing Catherine as he had seen Agnes in 1918, through the eyes of a love-sick adolescent: "either the writer is a simple fellow or she's Eleonora Duse disguised as a Red Cross nurse."[2]

Hemingway disagreed and let the characterization stand, only to have many of the critics echo the words of Fitzgerald. More than one critic observed that too often Hemingway's heroines seem to be the mere embodiment of male desire rather than fully developed three-dimensional characters. Indeed, Hemingway's most authentic female characters are the ones that come closest to imitating the masculine virtues which his heroes strive to practice. Thus Hemingway really saved his portrayal of Catherine by investing her with serenity and stability, qualities which show her to be a strong and resourceful individual who bolsters Frederic's will to face the misfortunes which dog their doomed relationship. The chaplain who often encourages Frederic to visit the wholesome mountain climate of his homeland in the Abruzzi, where

Frederic can get back to God and nature, is another source of inspiration for the novel's young hero. This priest also inspires Frederic to match the sort of self-giving love which Catherine nurtures for him by responding in kind, and in other ways influences the younger man who looks to him for direction.

If Frederic is the apprentice hero of the novel, the priest is the code hero of the story—in the sense of those terms previously elaborated. At their final meeting Frederic remarks, summing up the chaplain's train of thought, that one can grow spiritually as a result of accepting suffering and loss. "It is in defeat that we become Christian," he says. "I don't mean technically Christian. I mean like Our Lord."[3] It is these sentiments of stoic endurance and courage, one infers, that will ultimately enable Frederic to override the despair which engulfs him when Catherine dies in childbirth at the end of the novel and to realize that, as critic Arthur Waldhorn writes, to be loyal to one's beloved as Catherine was "is the only possible triumph."[4]

Frederic's initiation into a more mature, responsible attitude toward life and love involves a long and painful process for him in the course of the novel. It begins with his being wounded in battle and culminates in his desertion from the army during the chaos of the ignominious retreat from Caporetto, when the paranoid battle police are about to shoot him as a spy. It is as a fugitive, comments Robert Penn Warren, that Frederic learns the lesson of "lonely fortitude" which he will need in order to be able to reconcile himself to the final loss of Catherine in death.[5]

The novel ends with Frederic leaving Catherine's corpse behind in a darkened hospital room and walking home in the rain. Hemingway was always depressed by rain and frequently complained about it in his letters home from the front. In the novel he raised his natural dislike for rain to the symbolic level by making the deathly dark, relentless downpours that fall in several scenes, such as during the Caporetto retreat and

This publicity still was suggested by a scene in *A Farewell to Arms* (1932) in which Frank Borzage directed Helen Hayes as Catherine Barkley to "make love to the camera" for a shot photographed from the point of view of her lover, Frederic Henry (Gary Cooper). This is probably the only film ever to be released with alternate endings. (Courtesy of John Baxter)

Catherine's death struggle, signify the shadow of mortality that hovers over every human relationship. As Hemingway notes in the passage in *Death in the Afternoon* from which I have derived the epigraph of this book: "If two people love each other there can be no happy end to it."[6] Interestingly enough, Hemingway's rain symbolism was brought over into both the 1932 and 1957 film versions of the novel.

The success of the book when it appeared in 1926 almost assured that Hollywood would eventually want to film it. Laurence Stallings, co-author with Maxwell Anderson of the World War I drama *What Price Glory?*, had already dramatized *A Farewell to Arms* for Broadway, and though the run was short-lived, his version indicated the dramatic possibilities of the book for screen treatment. Hemingway, however, was not pleased that the film script would be drawn principally from Stallings's play rather than directly from the novel. He was likewise unhappy about the fact that Stallings would receive the same $24,000 fee for the screen rights to his play that he, Hemingway, would receive for the screen rights to the novel on which the play was based. Finally he was unhappy that according to the customary contractual arrangements governing movies sales of literary works, the film could be remade at a future date without any further recourse or emolument to the original author—which is precisely what happened a quarter of a century later.

Consequently, Hemingway was disgruntled about the whole project from the start. So far, his sole brush with Hollywood had been the sale of the title of his book of short stories *Men Without Women* to Twentieth Century-Fox for a submarine melodrama, and he ruefully began to wonder if he should have let his dealings with Hollywood go at that.

Paramount Pictures, the producing company of *Farewell*, thought of the film as a prestige production, however. The studio cast Gary Cooper and Helen Hayes in the leads, with distinguished character actors like Adolphe Menjou as Rinaldi in supporting roles, and named as director Frank Borzage, who had already established a solid reputation in Hollywood by winning Oscars for his direction of *Seventh Heaven* (1927) and *Bad Girl* (1931). The second unit director of the film was Jean Negulesco—later to direct a Hemingway film of his own, *Under My Skin* (1950)—who was responsible for the battle scenes. Negulesco remembers Borzage as a stickler for detail: in one crowded scene of epic proportions "all he was interested in was the way water would drip from a leaf and the way you'd see Gary Cooper passing by through this dripping water."[7]

Yet Borzage was not fundamentally a pretentious film-maker, for he believed that "the first duty of a director is to tell a story." He also felt that one of the duties of a director is "to make his pictures financially successful, which is another way of saying he must please his audience."[8] After the film was made, Hemingway thought that Borzage had tried too hard to please the mass audience and had really gone too far by providing alternate endings for the film, as we shall shortly see.

Another way in which the picture was tailored to avoid offending any segment of the mass audience was the suppression in the script of any of the book's criticism of the way the Italian army conducted its campaigns during the war, presumably to avoid a possible boycotting of the film by the Italian government or by Italian-Americans. The film in fact begins with a printed prologue which assures the audience that the Italian victory at the Piave River is inscribed "high on the rolls of glory," completely ignoring the wretched Caporetto retreat that preceded it.

Another way in which Borzage and his colleagues showed that they aimed to please their audience as much as possible was by refashioning Hemingway's love story along the lines of popular screen romance. Moviegoers of the period would not have approved of a heroine who too easily succumbed to a wartime romance with a soldier, so a scene was introduced into the film designed to establish Catherine from the outset as a young lady of sound character. In it Frederic meets Catherine for the first time in an air-raid shelter. He is still carrying the slipper of a prostitute from which he had been drinking champagne when the air-raid sirens sounded. Catherine has lost a shoe in the scuffle to get to the shelter in the dark, and in the darkness of the shelter Frederic drunkenly mistakes her for the other girl. He tries to put the gaudy slipper on her foot but it does not fit, just as she does not fit the category of the girl to whom it really belongs. Catherine, one is to infer, must be wooed and wed, not trifled with.

Not only audience expectations of conventional romantic movies but also the Motion Picture Code of the time dictated that Catherine and Frederic's relationship blossom into marriage, despite the incredible difficulties that a properly documented marriage would pose in a battle-torn country under enemy siege. The movie sidesteps this problem by dramatizing Catherine and Frederic's mutual willingness to marry in a scene in which the chaplain (Jack LaRue) reads the marriage ceremony for them at Frederic's hospital bedside, adding that "without the war you would have gotten married in God's grace."

But the most spectacular concession to the presumed demands of popular taste was, as I have said, the construction of two endings for the picture: one in which Catherine dies, as in the book, and another in which she apparently rallies and continues to live. In the first instance Frederic holds Catherine in his arms and reassures her that "we've never been apart since we met; we will never be apart in life or in death." She responds, "I believe it," and falls limp in his arms. With that, bells and whistles proclaim the Armistice and a flock of doves, symbolizing alike peace coming both to Catherine's liberated spirit and to the world at large, soars across the screen.

The alternate ending fades out on their embrace just as Catherine momentarily rallies in Frederic's arms, leaving the audience to assume, if they care to, that she will live. This assumption, of course, would undercut the twin symbolic implications of the title, according to which Frederic first bids farewell to military arms and then to Catherine's arms.

Exhibitors were advised that they could order either version of the ending for their theaters; but by all accounts most of them chose the original ending, since it was the one shown to the major critics and was favorably received by them. The alternate ending was selected only by a few small-town theater owners less sure of the sophistication of their patrons. In any event, the original ending was the one included in prints of the film circulated at the time of its rerelease in 1948 by Warner Brothers, who had obtained the rights to the picture in exchange for the rights to a novel which Paramount wanted to acquire from them. And that ending has been with the movie ever since.

Hemingway was apoplectic when he heard that two endings of the film were available to theaters at the time of its first release, and he publicly refused to see the picture at all—much less have the premiere in his wife's hometown of Piggott, Arkansas, while he was there visiting his in-laws. Given the adjustments made in his story to make it fit the conventional formulas of screen romance, his being upset was understandable, as was his intention to dissociate himself completely from the film.

Nevertheless there are some noteworthy things in the film, starting with the opening shot in which army vehicles can be seen moving slowly forward in the background, while the bandaged head of a dead soldier is visible in the foreground as mute testimony to the price paid for the advance taking place in the distance. By his deft use of a subjective camera at crucial moments, Borzage in the course of the film reminds the viewer that the story is being told from Frederic's point of view, as for example in the scene in which Frederic is transferred from an ambulance to a hospital bed. It is photographed totally from his point of view as the ceiling overhead rushes by while he is being transported along a hospital corridor into a room and lifted onto a bed, with various members of the hospital's medical staff peering down at him all the while.

The scene is climaxed by Catherine's appearance in the frame as she moves toward the bed and bends forward to kiss Frederic ecstatically. ("Make love to the camera," was Borzage's direction to Helen Hayes at this point.) This masterfully executed, uninterrupted traveling shot is topped off by the humorous touch of a nurse taking Frederic's temperature immediately after Catherine departs and observing with great concern that he is running a fever!

But none of Borzage's directorial touches would have served to mollify Hemingway, anymore than would the fact that the film was the biggest grosser of its year and went on to be nominated for best picture and to win Oscars for cinematography and sound recording. More than two decades later, just when Hemingway was beginning to feel that his novel's reputation had survived this initial attempt to bring it to the screen, he was chagrined to hear that producer David O. Selznick had purchased the screen rights from Warners and was bent on making his version of *A Farewell to Arms* the epic motion picture of World War I, just as his production of *Gone with the Wind* was the great cinematic epic of the Civil War. To this end Selznick hired Ben Hecht, one of the many uncredited scriptwriters who worked on *GWTW*, to do the screenplay.

Selznick's concept of making *Farewell* as a superspectacle not only ran counter to that of the spare 1932 version of the book, which got its story told in a compact eighty minutes, but also to Hemingway's own concept of his novel, which emphasized the personal love story of his principals more than the wartime background against which that story was set. There was danger that the more intimate dimension of the novel would be overwhelmed if the Selznick motion picture concentrated too much on elaborate and protracted battle scenes and other aspects of the war. Yet Selznick went ahead planning a super production to be shot on location in Europe.

One of the last of the old-fashioned Hollywood producers, David O. Selznick dominated every element of a film
while it was in production: he collaborated on the screenplay,
kibitzed on the direction of the film throughout the shooting
period, and supervised the postproduction work up to and
including the advertising campaign. He became increasingly
more dictatorial as he grew older, and this is clear from the
steady stream of memos which he compulsively churned out
while *Farewell* was in production, despite the fact that he had
engaged such respected movie veterans as Hecht to do the
screenplay and John Huston to direct.

Although, like Borzage, Selznick was convinced that his
first obligation was to the moviegoing public and not to
Hemingway, the screenplay which he and Hecht devised
stuck much more closely to the novel than the earlier, much
shorter film adaptation had done, even utilizing dialogue from
the book whenever possible. When Huston joined the venture, however, he suggested to Hecht several revisions which
would render the script even more faithful to Hemingway,
and then went off to Italy for preproduction preparations.

Angry at what he considered Huston's eleventh-hour
interference with the script, Selznick ordered most of
Huston's suggestions scrapped. In a sixteen-page, single-
spaced memo to Huston on the eve of the beginning of
principal photography in Italy, he berated the director for
trying to reinstate in the screenplay what he had earlier called
the "sloppy and careless" elements of Hemingway's handling
of his plot, which he and Hecht had labored so long to
eliminate. The novel, after all, was not "Holy Writ," and he
had no intention of becoming a "slave" to it. Selznick then
went on to carp about Huston's "wasting time" in rehearsing
scenes with the actors instead of concentrating on lining up
better location sites than he had already chosen. Unless
Huston were willing to submit to making the film according to
Selznick's dictates, the producer concluded, he would have no

choice but reluctantly to accept the director's resignation.[9] Huston walked off the picture and was replaced by Charles Vidor, a competent journeyman director whom Selznick could more easily dominate, but who was simply not in the same league with a director of Huston's caliber.

Selznick once explained that it was easier to criticize another man's direction of a film he was producing than to direct it himself, and his constant criticism of Vidor reached the point where late in the filming even this more pliable director shot off a memo warning Selznick that if he did not stop treating him as if he were a tyro, he, Selznick could finish the picture himself. The finished movie turned out to be closer to Hemingway's "Holy Writ" than the previous adaptation had been.

For one thing, the remake is at pains to indicate the positive influence of the chaplain (Alberto Sordi) on Frederic (Rock Hudson) in much the same way that the novel does and retains from the book some of their interchanges about life and love. In some ways the priest is even more of a code hero in the movie than he is in the novel. His nobility of character is brought into relief by an incident in which the chaplain stays behind with the wounded during the Caporetto retreat and is killed by an enemy shell while leading them in prayer. While it is not to be found in the novel, the chaplain's heroic death is completely in keeping with Hemingway's portrayal of the priest.

Moreover, although the heroism of other members of the Italian army is depicted in the Caporetto retreat sequence, the shameful mishandling of the retreat by the Italian officers in charge is not glossed over as it was in the 1932 movie. (A compensatory printed prologue at the beginning of the film assures the viewer that "no nation ever rose more gallantly out of defeat to victory.") Furthermore, the death of Catherine (Jennifer Jones) in childbirth is also portrayed in an uncompromising fashion and indeed ranks as one of the most harrowing childbirth sequences ever put on film.

Catherine Barkley (Jennifer Jones) and Frederic Henry (Rock Hudson) say farewell in the David O. Selznick remake of *A Farewell to Arms* (1957). Material from this novel was borrowed to fill out plot details in three other Hemingway films: *The Snows of Kilimanjaro*, *The Sun Also Rises*, and *Hemingway's Adventures of a Young Man*. (The Museum of Modern Art/Film Stills Archive)

Nonetheless, Selznick made some of the same kinds of commercial concessions to the public taste as Borzage had inserted. Selznick too included a spurious wedding scene in his film, but instead of having the chaplain preside over the ceremony at Frederic's bedside as in the earlier motion picture, Selznick has the lovers quietly exchange their proffered vows in the most unlikely of settings: at the racetrack amid the noisy jubilation that accompanies the announcement over the track's public address system of another Italian victory.

And just as Hemingway and anyone else familiar with

Selznick's penchant for spectacle could have prophesied, the producer beefed up the war scenes in his attempt to retool *A Farewell to Arms* into another *Gone with the Wind*, even modeling the Caporetto retreat after the burning of Atlanta sequence in the earlier movie, with hordes of Italian refugees trudging through the mud in the wake of the destruction they have left behind them. Although throughout the shooting period of *Farewell* Selznick continually reiterated in his memos that the love story should take precedence over the war story, the elaborate detail with which the lengthy scenes of spectacle were shot tends to weight the film down and cumulatively to overshadow the personal tragedy of Catherine and Frederic.

This is not to say that an epic episode like the Caporetto retreat is not skillfully done, for it includes compelling images of weary soldiers and wretched refugees plodding along together in the rain. But as novelist Philip Roth noted in his review of the film: "Naturalistic shots of barefoot tykes, pregnant women, squalling babies, call up pretty standard emotional reactions, and finally don't tell us much about the hero," who is participating in the retreat. The overall implications of this sequence seems to be that war is hell; but what gives significance to this episode in the novel, Roth contends, is that "this particular retreat is a particular kind of hell for a particular person."[10] And it is precisely the personal dimension of Frederic's own plight, as he tries to fight his way back to Catherine through the retreating hordes, that is obscured in this diffuse sequence. In the perspective of the film as a whole, then, these war scenes are really overblown set pieces which have been developed far beyond their function as plot devices in the story.

The picture is also marred, ironically enough, by too liberal a use of Hemingway's dialogue which, as has been noted, reads well on the printed page as highly wrought literary language but can for that very reason sound somewhat stilted when verbalized on the screen. Carefully crafted by Hemingway to illuminate Frederic's subjective psychological

states, the novel's interior monologues appear rather mannered when articulated by Rock Hudson on the screen. Thus
Frederic's ruminations about death and defeat in the final
hospital scene seems to be a genuine cry of anguish in the
book, but appear self-conscious and overwrought in the
movie.

This long speech, which includes Frederic's frank remark
that Catherine's ordeal is "the price you pay for sleeping
together," troubled Selznick because he feared that it might
cause censorship problems. The script at this point indicates
that the scene should be shot from several angles in order to
allow maximum flexibility in reediting the scene to meet
possible censorship demands.

Despite Selznick's concern about mollifying the guardi-
ans of film morality in this and other sequences, however, the
Legion of Decency, which rated films for its Catholic
constituency, designated the movie "morally objectionable in
part for all audiences" because in their view the film lacked a
sufficiently clear moral compensation for what the Legion
termed the picture's unrelieved emphasis on illicit love. Given
the fact that Catherine and her baby both die and that
Frederic is left desolate by the double loss, one wonders how
they could have arrived at this judgement. In any event,
because non-Catholics as well as Catholics often followed the
Legion's ratings at the time (since the industry was not to
provide the general public with a rating system for another
decade), *A Farewell to Arms* undoubtedly suffered at the box
office, to some degree at least, as a result of the Legion's
disapproving rating of the film.

Furthermore, the box-office potential of the film was not
helped by the fact that both of the principals were miscast, the
boyish Rock Hudson looking too young to play the worldly-
wise Frederic Henry, and Jennifer Jones at thirty-eight
looking too old to be a convincing Catherine. Although strong
performances were contributed by the distinguished Italian
actor-director Vittorio De Sica as Rinaldi and by other fine

supporting actors, the film could not survive the miscasting of the key roles.

When Selznick cabled Hemingway after the picture was finished that he planned to send the author $50,000 of the movie's eventual profits, even though Hemingway was not legally entitled to a nickel from the proceeds of the remake, the latter answered that he did not doubt but that a film which cast the nearly forty-year-old Mrs. Selznick as the twenty-four-year-old Catherine was probably doomed to financial disaster. He ungraciously suggested that if the movie should happen to turn a profit Selznick should have the $50,000 changed into nickels and "shove them up his ass until they came out his ears." Later, having walked out on a screening of the film after a half hour, Hemingway added that when a novelist sees a movie like the Selznick *A Farewell to Arms* made from a book that he is fond of, "it's like pissing in your father's beer."[11]

Even Selznick finally admitted his ultimate disappointment with the picture: "I frankly confess that, while a lot of people thought extremely highly of *A Farewell to Arms* it is not one of the jobs of which I am most proud."[12] Although there were to be more Hemingway film adaptations, *Farewell* was the last Selznick picture ever made. The movie did make a profit, though a small one; but the critical opprobrium heaped on his glossy, sprawling epic dogged his footsteps whenever he tried to secure funding for another film. David O. Selznick died in June 1965, characteristically leaving behind one last memo in which he dictated the details of his own funeral.

Hemingway had been so displeased with the 1932 screen adaptation of *Farewell*, especially because of the confusion about its multiple endings, that it was a decade before he sold the screen rights of another of his novels to Hollywood. That was his Spanish civil war novel, *For Whom the Bell Tolls*, which was filmed in 1943. An interesting companion piece to that movie is *The Spanish Earth*, a documentary film about the Spanish civil war on which Hemingway collaborated.

3
Death in the Afternoon of Life: *The Spanish Earth* (1937) and *For Whom the Bell Tolls* (1943)

Hemingway EMBARKED FOR SPAIN IN early 1937 to cover the civil war as a correspondent for the North American Newspaper Alliance and also to aid the Loyalist cause against the Fascist takeover of the government by collaborating on a documentary film entitled *The Spanish Earth*. The movie was being sponsored by a group of Loyalist sympathizers who called themselves Contemporary Historians, and who numbered among their ranks, besides Hemingway, novelist John Dos Passos, playwright Lillian Hellman, and poet Archibald MacLeish.

Prior to his working on *The Spanish Earth* Hemingway briefly helped Spanish novelist Prudencio de Pereda with the short propaganda film *Spain in Flames* (1937), but he was much more creatively engaged in the making of *The Spanish Earth*. The theme of the latter film was the attempt by Spanish peasants to cultivate their precious land in spite of the civil war raging all around them. Accompanying Dutch documentary filmmaker Joris Ivens and his cinematographer, John

Ferno, Hemingway roamed in and out of the combat zones, taking notes under fire on what the other two were photographing; these were for his future reference in composing the film's narration.

When shooting was completed, Hemingway told Ivens that he was willing to record the spoken commentary for the film himself, once the editing was completed, in order to ensure that his script would not be revised without his consultation during the postproduction work on the picture. Orson Welles recorded a trial run-through of the narration, but Ivens and the others finally decided that the voice-over commentary would have greater immediacy if Hemingway delivered it himself. And so it is the voice of Ernest Hemingway that is heard on the sound track of *The Spanish Earth*, even though to this day the opening credits of some prints of the film list Orson Welles as the commentator! It is a measure of Hemingway's commitment to the film that he agreed to record the commentary, since he harbored a lifelong fear of the microphone and later turned down endless offers to narrate television versions of his works.

When the film was completed, Hemingway and Ivens were invited by President Franklin D. Roosevelt to have the premiere at the White House, after which they moved on to California to screen the picture for the film colony in order to raise money for ambulances and medical supplies for the Loyalists. F. Scott Fitzgerald, who was present at one such gathering of movie people, later commented that Hemingway blew into Hollywood like a whirlwind and radiated an intensity that had "something almost religious about it," scooping up close to $14,000 in a single evening.[1]

Although *The Spanish Earth* is implicitly propagandistic in intent, Hemingway was too much of an artist not to focus his script much more on the human dimension of the situation in Spain than had been the case with the much more rabidly preachy *Spain in Flames*. (Even the contrasting tone of the titles of the two films illustrates the difference between them.) Indeed, one of the most convincing things about this documentary, remarked film critic Otis Ferguson, was "its abstention from bombast and sloganism. Much of the carrying power in understatement can be credited to Ernest Hemingway's commentary . . . With his knowledge and quiet statement of the odds against survival, that feeling for the people of Spain which comes from his heart, the combination of experience and intuition directing your attention quietly to the mortal truth you might well have missed in the frame, there could hardly have been a better choice."[2]

One undisputed virtue of Hemingway's script is his ability to personalize the Loyalist cause for the film audience by focusing on individuals within the groups of civilians and soldiers who are depicted within the course of the film. This artistic touch is grounded in the sound assumption that audiences cannot identify with an anonymous crowd of people on the screen, but only with individuals who are singled out as members of a group and who are representative of its other members. While Ivens trains his camera on the corpse of a civilian lying on a rubble-strewn sidewalk after a Fascist air assault on Madrid, Hemingway's voice explains stoically: "This is a man who has nothing to do with war. A bookkeeper on his way to his office at eight o'clock in the morning. So now they take the bookkeeper away, but not to his office or to his home." A coat has been thrown over the dead man's face as he becomes another of the faceless casualities of war.

Later the movie gains further dramatic focus by following a young Loyalist soldier named Julio home on a brief furlough to see his parents and to teach the local village males how to march and fire a rifle, in the event that they, like him, are called up to serve. Hemingway can even spare some sympathy for the Fascist dead, whether they be Spaniards or part of the German and Italian forces sent by Hitler and Mussolini to support Franco, their fellow Fascist. While the camera peruses the personal effects of a dead German pilot found in the wreckage of his plane and scans the faces of some dead Italian infantrymen, Hemingway notes: "We took no statements from the dead; but all the letters we read were sad."

The common humanity of those fighting on both sides of this dreadful conflict, which Hemingway so touchingly underscores in his script for *The Spanish Earth*, will be one of the pervasive themes of his great novel of the Spanish civil war, *For Whom the Bell Tolls*. He will, for example, draw on the episode in *The Spanish Earth* about reading the personal letters of dead enemy soldiers to build a poignant scene in the novel in which the hero reads a letter found in the pocket of a Fascist whom he has just killed—only to discover that the young man came from a pleasant little village with which he is familiar.

Yet Hemingway's powerful commentary remains unobtrusive throughout *The Spanish Earth* and perfectly complements the telling images which it accompanies. Perhaps the most memorable image in the entire film is that of the peasants stoically hoeing their beloved Spanish earth while the threatening rumble of guns thundering in the distance grows gradually louder, signaling that the war which threatens to destroy their land is moving steadily closer.

Nonetheless the documentary ends on a note of hope, as water floods through the irrigation ditches which the farmers have doggedly dug, refreshing the parched soil and thus symbolizing the rebirth of the land and of the nation once the hideous civil war has run its course. One is reminded of the epigraph which Hemingway borrowed from Ecclesiastes for *The Sun Also Rises* which states that, although generations come and go, "the earth abides forever."

After he completed his fund-raising tour with *The Spanish Earth* in the United States, Hemingway returned to Spain. A play entitled *The Fifth Column* was the creative fruit of his second expedition to Spain during the civil war, as *The Spanish Earth* had been the fruit of his first. The documentary movie was filmed under fire, and the play was written under fire.

Hemingway later recalled that while he was working on the play, the hotel in which he was staying in Madrid "was struck by more than thirty high explosive shells. So if it is not a good play perhaps that is what is the matter with it."[3]

The Fifth Column is in fact not a good play, and it was poorly received both when published in book form and when it made a brief and inauspicious appearance on Broadway in the spring of 1940 in a version revised by Hollywood screenwriter Benjamin Glazer, who had co-scripted the 1932 version of *A Farewell to Arms*. (Why Hemingway, who detested that film, consented to allow one of its perpetrators to tamper with his play no one, including Hemingway, has ever explained.) As a playwright Hemingway was a good novelist, creating dialogue which read much better on the page than it acted on the stage and which lacked the kind of dramatic intensity that generates theatrical excitement. As one theater critic noted: "The play has an unhappy way of standing still." Carlos Baker is right on target too when he notes that *The Fifth Column* did not then play, nor does it now read, like the work of an experienced playright. "For Hemingway's was not, in any sense that matters, a theatrical mind."

The most genuine and lasting fruit of Hemingway's civil war experiences was not his melodrama of counterespionage or even his documentary film, but his novel *For Whom the Bell Tolls*. By the time he began writing it at the end of 1938, the Loyalist cause was clearly lost, and he had become progressively disillusioned with what he termed "the carnival of treachery and rottenness on both sides."[4] That disillusionment would fall like a shadow across the pages of his novel; but the book would also be a salute to the indomitability of the human spirit, as was *The Spanish Earth*.

The play, which is a melodrama of counterespionage, has little in common with the novel except that the hero of both works is faced with the conflict of love versus duty. In the play Philip Rawlings gives up the girl he loves to carry on his work as a spy; in the novel Robert Jordan dies so that his beloved, and others too, might go on living and fighting for the Loyalist cause. But whereas Philip Rawlings is a sketchily drawn figure, Robert Jordan is a fully realized Hemingway apprentice hero in the tradition of Frederic Henry.

Superficially Jordan bears some resemblance to a member of the Loyalist Fifteenth International Brigade, Maj. Robert Merriman, an American economics teacher from a California college, while Jordan is a professor of Spanish literature from Montana. But like all Hemingway apprentice heroes Jordan's attitudes are fundamentally those of his creator. Like Hemingway, Jordan is more anti-Fascist than pro-Loyalist and he is aware that heroism and cruelty are displayed by individuals on both sides. "The political systems are rotten, but people who believe in them are, or can be, magnificent," writes Linda Wagner in summing up Hemingway's basically nonpartisan stance in the novel.[5] The novelist's clear-eyed objectivity, which enabled him to assess a political situation dispassionately, even while he was in the middle of it, of course stemmed from his experience as a journalist; and it is reflected in the fact that Hemingway saw no inconsistencey in maintaining his belief in Roman Catholicism, which he had embraced during World War I, despite the fact that the Church in Spain was officially endorsing Franco, simply because the issues at stake in the civil war were political and not religious. In one of the book's battle scenes the novelist makes this latter point by depicting soldiers in both armies petitioning the Blessed Virgin for help in winning the battle and praying afterward for the souls of their departed comrades.

For his part, Hemingway staunchly maintained that his ultimate allegiance was to the much exploited common people, as he had already demonstrated in *The Spanish Earth*, and it is a tribute to his objectivity that the book was attacked by partisans of both Fascist and Loyalist causes when it appeared, because neither group could claim it as coming out unequivocally in their favor. His novel was not a propaganda tract, after all, but a work of literature concerned with the universal theme of human brotherhood. The sentiments of the Russian Loyalist Karkov in the novel were Hemingway's own: "I am a journalist. But like all journalists I wish to write literature."[6]

The novel's theme is announced in the very title of the book, which refers to the epigraph taken from a sermon by the seventeenth-century poet-priest John Donne. In proclaiming that "no man is an island" separate from the shore, Donne is pointing up human interdependence. Hence, because each of us is involved with mankind, the death of any individual to some degree diminishes us all. Therefore, Donne concludes, when one hears a funeral knell, "never send to know for whom the bell tolls; it tolls for thee." In sum, human loss anywhere harms mankind everywhere.

This theme works itself out in the novel through Robert Jordan, an American expert in explosives, who joins a group of Loyalist guerrillas to help them launch an offensive by blowing up a crucial enemy bridge. His involvement with this small band grows during the brief time he is with them because they give him a sense of family feeling which he has never experienced before. Robert crowns his commitment to them by sacrificing his life so that they might escape the advancing enemy after the failure of their ill-conceived offensive.

In particular he feels united to Maria, the young refugee girl with whom he has fallen in love during his short sojourn with the guerrillas. He consolingly explains to her at the end that although his staying behind to cover the group's retreat will probably cost him his life, he and she have forged a mutual bond that will never be broken, and that "as long as there is one of us there is both of us."[7]

The code hero of this novel is the aging guerrilla Anselmo, who inspires the apprentice hero, Robert Jordan, in the same way that the chaplain in *A Farewell to Arms* served as an abiding inspiration for Frederic Henry. Anselmo looks upon all men as his brothers, including the enemy soldiers, and vows to do penance after the war in reparation for having had to take human life in battle. As he prepares to assist Robert in blowing up the bridge, he prays not for his own safety but that he will do his part in accomplishing their joint task. Then he sets off the charges and is himself killed in the blast.

Because Anselmo had become a surrogate father for Robert, his death is a tremendous loss for Robert. Physically short in stature, Anselmo is a spiritual giant and as such constitutes the moral norm of the novel. Before his tragic death he teaches Robert a great deal about the meaning of dedication to duty and of human comradeship. Indeed, it is perhaps the example of the selfless and self-effacing old man that more than anything else leads the wounded Robert to give his life for Maria and the others by holding off the enemy troops until his "family" can get away to safety.

Anselmo, moreover, reminds Robert of his revered grandfather who had fought in the American Civil War. And the combined inspiration which he derives from both men helps him to overcome the temptation to commit suicide, as his own father had, to escape his present pain and avoid capture. Robert knows that it is too late to save himself, but he can still do something to help the others. And so the novel ends with his resolution to last "until they come."[8] Robert's involvement with the band of guerrillas symbolizes his involvement with mankind. Hence his death affirms a universal brotherhood which transcends the boundaries of any single group or any individual cause, and in this way underscores the theme of the book.

Robert Jordan spoke in the course of the novel of writing a good and true book about his experiences in the Spanish civil war. But since he did not live to do it Hemingway did it for him, and the majority of the critics who did not have a political axe to grind agreed that Hemingway's book was both good and true. The question now was how much of that truth and goodness would find its way into the projected film version of the novel.

More than one literary critic had noticed that *For Whom the Bell Tolls* was as fitted for film adaptation as anything Hemingway had written up to that point: the entire novel takes place in a three-day time span and is organized around the central and climactic episode of the destruction of the bridge, the last symbolic link between the two warring factions; the exposition is primarily accomplished through action and dialogue; and there is enough "love interest" to attract moviegoers not otherwise interested in war stories. Not surprisingly, therefore, the sale of the screen rights to Paramount for close to $150,000 was completed a scant three days after the publication of the book in the fall of 1940. Because the sum he received represented the highest price paid for movie rights of a novel up to that point, Hemingway thought the deal "bloody wonderful."

Almost immediately nationwide speculation developed over the casting of the film's leads. Hemingway had recently met Gary Cooper and found him to be as impressive off-screen as on and therefore suggested him for the role of Robert Jordan. The pair subsequently established a life-long friendship and neither ever mentioned to the other the 1932 *A Farewell to Arms* in which Cooper had starred and against which Hemingway still harbored a grudge.

Cooper in turn introduced Hemingway to Ingrid Bergman, and the author was so impressed with her that he inscribed a copy of the novel to her as "the Maria of this story." Yet unaccountably the part originally went to the Norwegian-born actress Vera Zorina, whom director Sam Wood found unsuitable for the role after two weeks of shooting. Much to Hemingway's delight Wood asked for Bergman to replace Zorina.

Because in the story Maria's head has been shaved by the Fascists, Bergman would have to submit to a very close haircut. David O. Selznick, to whom Bergman was under contract, felt that the studio "had destroyed Zorina's looks with a murderous haircut" and therefore personally supervised the shearing of Bergman's hair for the role, which she took over the day after she finished shooting *Casablanca*.[9]

Paramount had initially considered the film as a possible project for C.B. DeMille and when the property was passed on to Sam Wood, he decided to make *For Whom the Bell Tolls* as much of a prestige picture as DeMille would have. In fact Wood wanted the movie to be the crowning achievement of his entire career. He not only replaced the leading lady two weeks into production but was willing to wait several months for Cooper to finish another film before beginning production in earnest in June 1942.

The exteriors were shot on location in the High Sierra Mountains in Northern California; Wood later recalled: "I never experienced anything as difficult as filming under the conditions we had, at an elevation of ten thousand feet, scrambling over rocks. We even uprooted wildflowers and greenery to prevent the harsh landscape from becoming 'pretty' for the technicolor camera; and we substituted ancient, gnarled tree trunks instead." In addition, the rocks were sprayed with a somber-hued paint to keep them from shining in the sunlight. "Not only did we go to the mountain," Wood concluded, "but we painted it too."[10]

Wood made good use of his locations during the shooting period, often photographing his players standing before the broad vistas or making their way through narrow mountain passes of the craggy mountains to give the audience a sense of the precarious, cliff-hanging existence of the guerrilla band. The company continued location shooting through the summer and returned to the studio in September for two months of shooting interiors.

The film had been scripted by Dudley Nichols, known for his work on such distinguished John Ford films as *The Informer* (1935) and *Stagecoach* (1939). When Hemingway was shown Nichols's adaptation, however, he was not pleased with it. Although the screenwriter had invested his scenario with more of the political implications of the novel than had Louis Bromfield's earlier version, Hemingway contended that the deep convictions which motivate Jordan to give his life for the Loyalist guerrillas were not sufficiently clear. He also felt that the guerrillas themselves were depicted as belonging in a "fourth-rate production of Bizet's *Carmen*" or a pseudo-Spanish Hollywood epic like *The Mark of Zorro* rather than in a serious film about the Spanish civil war. Hemingway insisted, among other things, that to reflect their native simplicity and dignity they be dressed in grays and blacks—and without the garish red bandannas called for in Nichols's script.[11]

Whereas in Selznick's 1957 *A Farewell to Arms* the war story would be emphasized over the love story, in the present instance the emphasis was completely reversed. Aside from a short speech late in the movie, in which Robert Jordan indicates that one of his reasons for fighting in Spain is that the Nazis and other Fascists are using the civil war as a dress rehearsal for a full-scale war in Europe, there remains relatively little reference in the film to the political situation underlying the Spanish civil war, despite Hemingway's criticism of the script on this point. Wood responded to this objection that the political issues had been fogged over in the movie by simply saying: "It is a love story against a brutal background. It would be the same love story if they were on the other side."[12] It is probably closer to the truth that since the Fascists under Franco had won the civil war and were now in power in Spain producer-director Wood and the studio bosses wanted to soft-pedal the political implications of the story in order to avoid running the risk of having the film boycotted by the Spanish government or by Spanish groups in the United States—just as the same studio's officials had worried about offending Italians with the 1932 version of *A Farewell to Arms*.

In addition to coping with the political dimension of Hemingway's novel in the film, the moviemakers faced other difficulties in bringing the book to the screen. Although the novel is not narrated in the first person by the hero, as was *A Farewell to Arms*, the story is nevertheless told for the most part from Jordan's point of view and often gives his subjective reactions to what is happening. But it is difficult to suggest in a film that the story is being told from the subjective point of view of one of the characters, aside from including occasional subjective camera shots from the main character's point of view, as Borzage did in his *A Farewell to Arms*, or having the central character's voice surface on the sound track from time to time as narrator, as in the Selznick *Farewell*.

"One cannot tell a story from the single point of view of one character in a film as one can in a novel," Graham Greene once explained. "You cannot look through the eyes of one character in a film." It is true that the central character remains on the screen more than anyone else in the movie, Greene continued, and his comments are often there on the sound track. "But we still do not see others completely from his point of view as we do in the novel."

Thus Anselmo appears as a likeable and decent old man in the movie but the viewer never grasps the extent to which he is a source of inspiration for Jordan, because Jordan's internal thoughts about Anselmo's sage reflections on life are not in the film. Similarly, no attempt was made to include in the film Jordan's interior monologues centering around his recollections of his father and grandfather. Therefore the last scene of the movie, in which Jordan waits for the enemy to come into the range of his machine gun, is robbed of some of the emotional conflict which he experiences at this point in the book. In the scene as Hemingway wrote it there is an interior monologue in which Jordan must overcome the temptation to follow his father's example and commit suicide; he opts instead to face this last challenge of his life in keeping with the example set by his grandfather and by Anselmo.

The movie makes a stab at simulating Jordan's final internal monologue—the only such attempt in the entire movie—by having his voice heard on the sound track, spurring himself on to remain conscious long enough to cover the guerrilla's retreat by thinking of Maria. Then he shouts, "Now they can't stop us ever. She's going on with me!" and opens fire right at the camera. The screen clouds with gunsmoke which evaporates to show a huge bell tolling, as the movie comes to an end. An effective finale, but it lacks the extra dimension of the complex psychological conflict rooted in Jordan's past which Hemingway brought to bear in the last pages of the book.

Another problem with which the filmmakers had to cope was the handling of what one might call the "external monologues" in the novel, that is, the episodes in which Pilar, a female member of the guerrilla band (Katina Paxinou), and Maria recount for Jordan their memories of atrocities which took place earlier in the war. Since Maria's recollections involved her brutal gang rape by a group of Fascists, Wood elected to have her recount these events to Jordan without portraying them in flashback, since the Production Code prohibited their being visualized on the screen and audience sensibilities at the time would probably have recoiled from watching a direct presentation of this material.

Conversely, Wood decided to depict in flashback Pilar's account of the execution of some captured Fascists by a band of Loyalist guerrillas, Pilar serving as the narrator on the sound track. This was a wise decision since, as Claude-Edmonde Magny comments in her book on the film aesthetic of fiction, this flashback helps in the movie, just as Pilar's narration of the event helps in the novel, to present "a kind of fresco" of the Spanish civil war which enlarges the frame of reference in which the individual lives of the characters are being presented.[13]

Regrettably this is one of the sequences which Wood shortened when he cut the film by some thirty minutes for its second release, because many critics had complained about the film's length during its initial run. By and large, however, the film was a success and it garnered Academy Award nominations for best picture, cinematography, art direction, editing, musical score, as well as acting nominations for Cooper, Bergman, Paxinou, and Akim Tamiroff (as Pablo, a guerrilla leader). Although only Katina Paxinou won an Oscar, the multiple nominations indicate that Wood had brought out the best in his collaborators, though he himself, much to his disappointment, did not get nominated.

Robert Jordan (Gary Cooper) and Maria (Ingrid Bergman) in the famous sleeping-bag sequence from *For Whom the Bell Tolls* (1943). The scene was thought daring for its time, but Hemingway wondered how Cooper could make love without removing his coat. (Courtesy of John Baxter)

The picture was one of the top grossers of 1943, moreover, and its box-office potential was aided considerably by the celebrated love scene in which Cooper and Bergman snuggle together in his sleeping bag on a spring night. Since in the forties the Production Code forbade a couple being shown together in the same bed, the sleeping bag love scene was thought to be quite daring for its time. But the scene was too tame for Hemingway, who chuckled about the absurdity of Cooper having to make love to Bergman without even removing his coat.

Though Hemingway admired the performances of Cooper and Bergman, as Carlos Baker notes, in general the novelist thought that the film did not sufficiently reflect the grim atmosphere in which Jordan and the guerrillas had to exist. Mary Hemingway remembers his laughing about "Coops climbing the mountain to join the guerrillas in that brand-new shirt from Abercrombie and Fitch."[14] Still it is hard to believe that the movie would have been better had it been machine-tooled into a DeMille spectacle. In addition, Stuart Kaminsky reports in his book on Cooper that Hemingway's serious and sincere comment to Cooper about his portrayal of Jordan was this: "You played Robert Jordan just the way I saw him, tough and determined. Thank you."

4
A Man Alone:
To Have and Have Not (1944),
The Breaking Point (1950),
and *The Gun Runners* (1958)

THE PRESENCE OF ERNEST HEMINGWAY STILL pervades Key West, Florida, where he went to live with his second wife, Pauline, in 1928 and maintained a house for three decades, even after he twice remarried and took up official residence in Cuba in the forties and fifties. Today the Hemingway house in Key West is a museum where one can see mementoes of the novelist's life and work. It stands a few blocks away from Sloppy Joe's Bar, which sports a sign over the entrance that proudly proclaims it to have been Hemingway's favorite tavern during his Key West years. Inside, enshrined on a wall near the bar, hangs a large photograph (a copy of which looks down on me as I write) of Hemingway sipping a mug of beer. Sloppy Joe's was also a favorite of Harry Morgan, the hero of Hemingway's Key West novel *To Have and Have Not* (1937), though it is "disguised" as Freddie's Bar in the novel.

To Have and Have Not, the single Hemingway novel set in his homeland, began its artistic life as a short story entitled

"One Trip Across," about a smuggling expedition of rum runner Harry Morgan (named for the famous buccaneer) off the coast of Key West. This story was followed by a companion piece called "The Tradesman's Return," and Hemingway then decided to lump the two stories together as the first two sections of a novel about Morgan, to which he added a third, longer segment designed to round off the account of Harry's life. The novelist failed to weave a sufficient amount of narrative unity into the fabric of the book, however. Unfortunately the seams still clearly show in the finished work, and the book remains a patchwork job, made up of three clearly definable episodes which do not add up to a coherent, artistic whole.

In the last, longest section Hemingway introduced several minor characters who represented the affluent "haves" that were meant to serve as a contrast to the struggling "have nots," embodied by Harry and his wife and two daughters. Their function is to provide social comment on the inequities of a social system under which Harry is forced to employ his fishing launch for smuggling contraband cargo in order to support his family during the Depression, while the idle rich lounge on their yachts in leisure and luxury.

But social comment was never Hemingway's strong suit, and the real theme that emerges from the book is a much broader one, articulated by Harry as he lies near death in the wake of a shootout with some Cuban revolutionaries; namely, that "a man alone ain't got no bloody fucking chance."[1] It is, of course, but a short step from Harry's dying words to the epigraph of *For Whom the Bell Tolls*, written immediately after *To Have and Have Not* but filmed before it. Too late Harry has realized that "no man is an island," that he has needed others just as they have needed him. This theme, moreover, appealed to the director of the first adaptation of the novel, Howard Hawks, as much as it did to Hemingway, for comradeship is an important element in the Hawksian universe.

Hawks was known for making films that did not get bogged down in "significant" dialogue, but told their stories in a straightforward fashion that nonetheless implied subtle thematic implications beneath the surface of their basically action-oriented plots. Hawks always worked on the scripts of his films, whether he got screen credit for doing so or not. Over the years, he developed the custom of sitting down with a pad of yellow paper each morning before shooting began to change any dialogue that no longer seemed to fit the flow of the film as it had been progressing. "I change the dialogue to fit the action," he explained. "I don't really improvise."

Script troubles abounded on *To Have and Have Not*, even though the screenplay was credited to veteran screenwriter Jules Furthman, who had done several films for Hawks, and to William Faulkner, Hemingway's only serious contemporary rival as a major American novelist. Indeed, *To Have and Have Not* represents the only time in film history that two Nobel Prize winners were involved in the same film story: Hemingway and Faulkner. Hawks recalled the genesis of the first film version of *To Have and Have Not* for me this way:

"I tried to get Ernest Hemingway to write for pictures as Bill Faulkner had done for me on several occasions, but Hemingway said that he was going to stick to the kind of writing that he knew best. Once, on a hunting trip, I told him that if he would give me the worst story that he had ever written, we would make a good movie out of it. He asked me what I thought was his worst novel and I said *To Have and Have Not*, which I thought was a bunch of junk. He said that he had written it when he needed money and that he didn't want me to make a movie out of it. But finally he gave in."

While they continued their hunting expedition, Hawks and Hemingway discussed the project, and Hawks convinced Hemingway that the most screenworthy part of the book was the first section, which consisted essentially of the short story "One Trip Across," in which Harry Morgan becomes enmeshed in smuggling some aliens out of revolution-torn Cuba.

To fill out the plot the script would draw on later portions of the novel as well, but Hawks told Hemingway that he also wanted the screenplay to include some events that actually took place before the beginning of the novel, such as Harry's meeting and falling in love with Marie, to whom he has already been married several years at the point when the novel begins.

In point of fact Hemingway had earlier sold the screen rights of the novel for $10,000 to producer Howard Hughes, who had never come up with a viable screenplay. Hughes demanded and got $92,000 for the screen rights to the book from Warner Brothers, who agreed to finance and distribute the film which was being made by Hawks's independent unit at the studio. Because of his quarter share in the movie's profits, Hawks eventually made more than ten times the latter amount on the film. Later, when he revealed these figures to Hemingway, the novelist "didn't speak to me for three months."

Jules Furthman did an initial scenario along the lines of the screen treatment which Hawks had discussed with Hemingway. When Hawks submitted this version of the script to the Office of the Coordinator of Inter-American Affairs, however, he was advised that the State Department feared that a motion picture which depicted insurrection and smuggling in Cuba would place a strain on Cuban-American relations and the United States could not afford to alienate an ally while World War II was still being waged.

Warner Brothers did not want to risk having the Office of Inter-American Affairs deny the film an export license, which would mean that the movie could not be exhibited outside the United States and would automatically forfeit a significant portion of its potential profits. Hawks therefore decided to situate the setting of the film in wartime Martinique, a French island under the control of the pro-Nazi Vichy government, which was completely beyond the diplomatic jurisdiction and concerns of the Office of Inter-American Affairs.

According to Bruce Kawin's carefully researched introduction to the published screenplay of *To Have and Have Not*, it was Faulkner who suggested at this point that the story could be altered so that Harry Morgan would become involved in smuggling anti-Vichy Free French adherents of General de Gaulle instead of Cuban revolutionaries. During his sojourn at Warner's the previous year Faulkner had researched and written an unproduced screenplay about General de Gaulle and was therefore already familiar with the milieu of the revised story line of *To Have and Have Not*. Hawks therefore gave Faulkner, who had recently been assigned to work on the film adaptation, the go-ahead to refashion Furthman's screenplay accordingly.

Furthermore, the switch in the story's setting enabled Hawks to have the revised screenplay model the role of Harry Morgan, to be played by Humphrey Bogart, after the part of Rick which Bogart had played in Warners' hugely successful movie of the previous year, *Casablanca*, so that in the later film the Bogart character would once again be helping Free French Resistance fighters escape the clutches of the Nazis. Hawks obviously hoped that his film would repeat the success of its predecessor.

The upshot of all of these substantial changes in the plot of the movie was that the screenplay was getting farther and farther away from Furthman's first draft, which had been worked out more or less according to the preliminary treatment that Hawks had originally sketched out for Hemingway. While the sets were being rebuilt to fit the movie's new locale, Faulkner had to work against time to get as much of the revised script written as soon as possible before the start of principal photography. Once shooting had started, he found himself working out a scene only a couple of days before it was scheduled to go before the camera. Faulkner wrote to his agent, Harold Ober, on April 22, 1944, that he had started work on *To Have and Have Not* on February 22 and that Hawks had started shooting at the beginning of March.

"Since then I have been trying to keep ahead of him with a day's script."[2]

At times Hawks, with his ever-present pad of yellow paper, would revise snatches of dialogue with the aid of the actors on the set; at other times Faulkner would take the freshly mimeographed pages of a scene that he was not satisfied with right to the sound stage and put the finishing touches on the dialogues in tandem with director and cast. Faulkner seems to have enjoyed these give-and-take sessions very much, for he later said that "the moving picture work which seemed best to me was done by the actors and the writer throwing the script away and inventing the scene in actual rehearsal just before the camera turned."[3]

While it is clear from a perusal of the final shooting script that Faulkner and the others hardly "threw the script away," it is also true that this kind of improvising yielded some memorable bits of dialogue, as evidenced by the fact that some of the nifty lines which one hears spoken on the screen are not in the final shooting script and therefore must have been invented on the set. For example, right after Morgan insists to his new girl friend Marie (Lauren Bacall) that there are no strings attached to him because he does not make personal or political commitments of any kind, he hears that his best friend Eddy (Walter Brennan) is in the hands of the Gestapo-like Vichy police. As he runs from Marie's hotel room to go to Eddy's aid, she calls after him, "Don't trip on the strings on your way downstairs." This dandy payoff line does not appear in the final printed script and is, incidentally, as close as the Hawks version of *To Have and Have Not* comes to expressing explicitly the conviction of Harry Morgan at the end of the novel that "a man alone has no . . . chance."

Another interesting sample of the teamwork that characterized the working out of the screenplay of this movie revolves around the scene in which Bacall made movie history in this, her very first film, by telling Bogart that if he wanted anything, all he had to do was whistle: "You know how to whistle, don't you? Just put your lips together and blow." About this scene Hawks recalled: "I wrote that line as part of her screen test and it went over so well that Jack Warner, the head of the studio, insisted that we find a place to put it into the picture. Faulkner decided to put it in while Bacall was standing at the doorway of Bogart's hotel room with no one else around, so that the audience wouldn't miss the implication." They didn't then and don't now.

Faulkner was good at creating dialogue, but sometimes he got carried away and would write a lengthy scene which would be fine for a novel but wrong for a film. On one occasion he showed up on the set with a six-page speech for Bogart to learn. The actor examined the material and ruefully inquired: "I'm supposed to say all that?" Hawks intervened and assured both men that the scene could be cut down to size without doing violence to its meaning.

Faulkner was the first to admit that Jules Furthman had a way of telegraphing a great deal to the audience with little or no dialogue at all. In Furthman's original draft of the screenplay, which served as the basis for the Faulkner rewrite, he suggested the kind of girl that Marie was, and how Harry would react to her accordingly by this unspoken interchange: "She looks at Harry to light her cigarette. Harry looks at her for a minute, sizes her up, then tosses her the matches to light her own cigarette."

Although the Bogart-Bacall team struck cinematic sparks in *To Have and Have Not*, the film really belongs to Bogart, who is able to show in his performance how Harry develops by film's end into a typical Hawksian hero: a man who achieves self-respect by stoically maintaining his personal integrity. In Hawks's male universe, as in Hemingway's, the virtues most prized are courage and loyalty to one's duty and to one's comrades. Hence the Hawksian hero has much in common with the Hemingway code hero, and Harry Morgan can easily be identified as either.

Harry becomes increasingly aware in the film, just as he

does in the novel, of his need for male comradeship, represented by his sidekick Eddy, and for female companionship, represented by Marie, implicitly realizing that "a man alone has no . . . chance." Furthermore, despite the fact that in the past Harry has consistently refused to commit himself to any cause, he eventually decides, because of his growing kinship with others, to help the Free French at the cost of grave personal peril because his own stubborn sense of independence is revolted by the cruel tactics employed by the agents of the Vichy government in tracking down the Free French fugitives. When one of the latter asks why Harry has finally agreed to aid them, Harry answers laconically: "Because I like you and I don't like them." Beneath Harry's tough exterior, Bogart neatly implies in his performance, is a humanity that can be touched.

One of the incidents that appears in both the book and the film which illustrates that Harry is both a code hero and a Hawksian hero concerns Mr. Johnson (a "have") engaging Harry (a "have not") to take him fishing for a couple of weeks. In the course of the trip Johnson allows Harry's expensive fishing gear to be lost overboard because of his careless and cowardly handling of a big marlin which he fails to land. Johnson balks at paying for the loss of the equipment at the end of the trip and ultimately swindles Harry out of the whole amount which he owes him for the two-week fishing trip by leaving town without paying him a cent.

Johnson's behavior bears out Hemingway's previously noted conviction that when a man cheats at sports as Johnson did in the shabby way he handled the big fish, he is unlikely to live up to his obligations in other areas of his life. Conversely, Harry demonstrates the code by which he lives both in trying to get Johnson to capture the marlin fairly and humanely and in playing square with him in assessing what Johnson owes him. In moral terms, then, Johnson is a "have not" and Harry is a "have," their social and financial status in reverse.

Despite the parallels between the typical Hawksian hero

Lauren Bacall and Humphrey Bogart struck cinematic sparks as Marie and Harry in Howard Hawks's *To Have and Have Not* (1944). William Faulkner co-authored the screenplay, making this film the only one in the history of motion pictures to be the creative product of two Nobel Prize winners, Hemingway and Faulkner. (Warner Brothers)

From left to right: Harry Morgan (Humphrey Bogart), Marie (Lauren Bacall), and Frenchy (Marcel Dalio) express concern for a wounded French Resistance fighter. By some coincidence Marcel Dalio played the role of a French barkeep in three Hemingway films: here in *To Have and Have Not,* and in *The Snows of Kilimanjaro* and *The Sun Also Rises.* (Warner Brothers)

Harry Morgan (John Garfield) and Leona Charles (Patricia Neal) in the first remake of *To Have and Have Not,* Michael Curtiz's *The Breaking Point* (1950). *To Have and Have Not* was remade again in 1958 as *The Gun Runners,* directed by Don Siegel and starring Audie Murphy. (Museum of Modern Art/Film Stills Archive)

and the typical Hemingway code hero which can be found in comparing book and film, many film critics voiced their disappointment that the movie was in some ways more like *Casablanca* than it was like Hemingway's novel. For one thing, they rejected as spurious Hawks's claim that in the movie he showed how Harry and Marie met and fell in love long before they became the middle-aged couple of Hemingway's book. But at forty-five Humphrey Bogart was already twice the age of newcomer Lauren Bacall (though they were soon to be married), while the Harry and Marie of the novel are both in their mid-forties. This age discrepancy aside, however, it is not implausible to think that the sleek and seductive Marie of the film could have developed in middle age into the more amply built, lusty Marie of the novel and that the Harry Morgan of the movie could have quite credibly become in later life the more hardened and embittered, though no less courageous man which the novel shows him to be.

Taken strictly on its own merits, *To Have and Have Not* is a popular and entertaining motion picture with lots of action and suspense and some Hoagy Carmichael songs sung by him and by Lauren Bacall (there is no factual justification to the rumor that Bacall's songs were dubbed by Andy Williams, though Pauline Kael and other critics have perpetuated this myth in writing about the movie). In any event, the movie sent people back to the book since the Grosset and Dunlap tie-in edition of the novel went through three printings during the period in which the film was in general release.

Hawks conceded that after his adaptation of *To Have and Have Not* there was still enough material from the book to serve as the basis of at least one more film version of the novel. In fact there were to be two remakes of *To Have and Have Not*, the first of which was Michael Curtiz's *The Breaking Point* (1950). The impetus behind this second screen version of the novel, according to Frank Laurence's unpublished thesis on Hemingway and film, was screenwriter Ranald MacDougall, who convinced Warner executives that a screenplay that was more faithful to the book and had less in common with *Casablanca* could be just as viable as the Hawks version had been. There was unconscious irony in the choice of Michael Curtiz, who had directed *Casablanca*, to direct *The Breaking Point*. But this was all to the good since, having made *Casablanca* once, he was as interested as MacDougall in making a movie that stuck to Hemingway's story line and was not in any way similar to *Casablanca*.

Nonetheless there was bound to be some overlap between the Hawks and the Curtiz films of Hemingway's novel, and both movies begin by covering Johnson's swindle of Harry and Harry's consequent need to earn money by smuggling passengers on his charter boat. But even here differences between the two films crop up.

The Curtiz movie changed the setting of the story yet again, this time to a small California town a few years after the war, where Harry Morgan (John Garfield) is involved in smuggling Chinese aliens, as in the book. Secondly, Eddy, Harry's buddy in the Hawks film, is replaced in *The Breaking Point* by a black named Wesley (Juano Hernandez), another friend of Harry's in the novel. Thirdly, the Curtiz film gives Johnson (called Hannagan in the second film) a girl friend, Leona Charles (Patricia Neal), who accompanies them on the fishing trip on Harry's boat. Her function seems to be to make a play for Harry in much the same way that the Bacall character does in the Hawks motion picture, with the crucial difference that Harry has a wife, Lucy (Phyllis Thaxter), and two daughters in the second film—as he does in the novel—and he discourages Leona's advances.

The Breaking Point goes on to develop the last and longest section of the novel, which was hardly touched upon in the Hawks movie. Harry agrees to use his boat as the means of escape for a mob planning a big robbery; but the movie avoids the political implications of the novel by making the robbers American mobsters, rather than Cuban revolutionaries stealing money to support their cause.

To avoid a loss of audience sympathy for Harry, the movie goes to a great deal of trouble to demonstrate that he is driven to act as an accessory to robbery solely for the sake of bailing his family out of debt. This is established in a montage sequence in which Harry reduces the daily rate for renting his charter boat from $40 to $25, and his wife is shown working far into the night earning money by mending sails while Harry guiltily lies awake nearby. Harry is placed in a still more favorable light in the film by his decision to disassociate himself from the mobsters by turning them in to the police for the reward.

The gangsters suspect that this is what he plans to do, but in the ensuing shootout aboard his launch he manages to gun down all four mobsters, but not before they kill Wesley and seriously wound him. As he is being placed in an ambulance at dockside to be rushed to the hospital, Harry deliriously mutters to his wife the story's thematic statement that a man alone has no chance. In the book Harry dies after uttering this statement, but the movie ends ambiguously with Lucy assurring her daughters that their father will pull through if they pray for him.

Ranald MacDougall told Frank Laurence that he wanted to end the film in the same way that the book does, with Harry's wife being informed of her husband's demise. But producer Jerry Wald and Curtiz—in a departure from his insistence on a faithful screen treatment of the novel—opted for the ending of the film as it stands. The conclusion as shot is an obvious concession to the old Hollywood taboo against potentially offending the mass audience by allowing unhappy endings in which the hero did not survive. The box office success of a film like *For Whom the Bell Tolls*, in which the hero dies at the end of the movie, was looked upon as an exception to the rule and did not wipe away the taboo.

Yet, in fairness to Curtiz and Wald, one must concede that the movie's finale *is* ambiguous and the viewer *is* free to infer that Harry's life has come to a tragic close just as Hemingway meant it to. In fact, "it was Ranald MacDougall's intention that the audience understand that Morgan will die," Laurence writes; and MacDougall sought to "encourage" the audience to grasp this implication both by dialogue and visual imagery.[4]

Asked by a reporter if Harry is seriously wounded, a Coast Guard officer replies, "From what they tell me, he's so close to being dead it doesn't matter." What's more, the closing image of the film is a shot of Wesley's son standing on the pier waiting for news of his father, who he does not yet know is dead. The point of this image, which many reviewers missed, was that it is only a matter of time before Harry's wife and children hear of his inevitable death, just as Wesley's boy will surely learn of his father's murder.

Although the moviemakers hedged their bets by making Harry a more sympathetic hero than Hemingway did and by supplying a potentially more comforting ending, *The Breaking Point* remains one of the more faithful transcriptions of a Hemingway book to film. Unfortunately it has been overshadowed by the more popular Hawks adaptation and continues to be virtually ignored. However, George Morris contends in his book on John Garfield that this film represents the summit of the actor's career and one of Curtiz's finest achievements.

Curtiz's assured direction of the picture is evidenced in his careful choice of lighting effects and visual symbolism. For example, the inner corruption of the shyster lawyer Duncan (Wallace Ford), who serves as liaison between Harry and the mob, is ironically pointed up by dressing him in white, the conventional sign of purity and innocence. Curtiz indicates Duncan's association with shady deals by lighting his discussions with Harry and the gangsters about the robbery in sinister semi-darkness and shadows. The darkness hovering around Harry and the others as they discuss their scheme with Duncan seems to be waiting to engulf them all in the violent climax of the film.

"*The Breaking Point* is all too little appreciated," comments film critic Richard Lillich. "It dug into human motives and made real-life problems exciting."[5] MacDougall notes that Hemingway said that the movie "suited him,"[6] despite the fact that he received no financial compensation from the remake of *To Have and Have Not* since he had originally sold the screen rights of the book outright and had no control over their subsequent resale.

When, however, he learned in 1958 that his book was to serve as the basis of yet another film, and this time a low-budget second feature updated in setting to cash in on the current world interest in the Castro revolt in Cuba, he was decidedly unhappy. As an alien resident, he was eager to stay out of the island's tricky and volatile political situation. He had little use for the soon-to-be-ousted dictator, Batista; nevertheless, he did not want his name associated with a film that could be construed as a "piece of propaganda for Castro."[7]

Chagrin turned to outrage, therefore, when starlet Gita Hall announced that she was planning to change her name to Gita Hall Hemingway to indicate her lasting pride at being linked with a movie made from one of this great writer's books. Hemingway's lawyers put a stop to this painfully obvious publicity ploy, but could not put a stop to the making of the film, to be called *The Gun Runners*.

Director Don Siegel was reluctant to make a film of a story that had been filmed twice before, "particularly when the other two versions were so good." However, he "needed the money." A first version of the script had been prepared by Ben Hecht, who had just done the screenplay for the 1957 remake of *A Farewell to Arms*. His work was revised by Paul Monash, and Siegel did further rewriting in collaboration with Daniel Mainwaring in an attempt to bring the screenplay more into line with the novel. The finished script emerged as a curious amalgam of some elements from the novel mixed together with newly invented ingredients, as well as some lifted from *The Breaking Point*.

Because of the change of the setting to the time of Castro's revolution, some of the original dialogue from the novel referring to the Cuban revolution of the thirties is retained in *The Gun Runners* and made to refer to the current political situation—although Castro's name is never mentioned in the film. Thus, when the Cuban revolutionaries approach the hero of the film, now called Sam Martin (Audie Murphy), while he is visiting in Havana and ask him to smuggle some refugees for them, Sam replies with a brittle line that is verbatim from the book: "I don't care who is president here. But I don't carry anything to Key West that can talk."

The villain of *The Gun Runners* is Hanagan (not to be confused with Hannagan, the name given the Johnson character in *The Breaking Point*). Because of Sam's financial straits, Hanagan (Eddie Albert) is able to press-gang Sam into transporting to Havana the weapons he is selling illegally to the Cuban revolutionaries. Hanagan has no counterpart in the novel, nor does his mistress, Eve, who seems to be modeled on the Leona Charles character of *The Breaking Point* and is no more successful in luring Sam away from his wife than is her counterpart in the film.

The Siegel film suffered not only from being a curious mishmash of elements from the Hemingway book and the Curtiz version but from a meager twenty-day shooting schedule which did not allow the director enough time to give it the professional look he wanted it to have. Moreover, when the producer saw that the schedule was almost used up, he insisted that the movie be finished on time. Scott Hale, the dialogue director on the film, recalls that "since the picture was being shot in continuity, from beginning to end, Don in desperation simply had Audie kill everybody; and that was the end of the picture."[8]

The gun battle which hurriedly finishes off both the villains and the movie is precipitated by the discovery en route to Cuba that Hanagan's gun crates are in fact filled with rocks. Sam reasons that Hanagan will murder him to keep him quiet, and in self-defense he kills off Hanagan and his henchmen, himself escaping with only a flesh wound. He is last seen docking in Key West, where his smiling and beautiful wife anxiously awaits him on shore. The undiluted happy ending of the film is in keeping with the lightweight tone of the entire picture.

Although Hemingway's Harry Morgan is admittedly not a prime example of one of the author's code heroes, he nevertheless qualifies for that status; and in both the Hawks and the Curtiz films Harry Morgan's character more or less corresponds to that of the novel's code hero. But throughout *The Gun Runners* Sam Martin is presented as a one-dimensional romantic movie hero who has little in common with the Harry Morgan of either the book or the previous two films. Given Audie Murphy's uninspired performance, one wonders if he could have played a character as complex as Hemingway's Harry. His limited ability was especially pointed up when it was measured against the performance of such seasoned actors as Eddie Albert and Everett Sloane, who played Sam's sidekick. "I'm working under a handicap," Murphy once confided to a film director. "I have no talent." This disarming candor did not improve his performance, however, and his portrayal of the key role in *The Gun Runners* further weakened the movie.

The Gun Runners was little more than a crass exploitation of the Hemingway book, which did little credit to anyone associated with it. Siegel was later to direct another Hemingway film, *The Killers* (1964), a remake of Robert Siodmak's movie of the same short story. In comparing these two film versions of the same Hemingway story in the next chapter, the hazards of stretching a short story into a feature-length film will be brought into relief, for Hemingway's story provided only the opening sequence for these two vastly different movies.

5
Growing Pains:
The Killers (1946 and 1964) and *Hemingway's Adventures of a Young Man* (1962)

DURING HIS EARLY YEARS, HEMINGWAY WAS unconsciously storing up experiences that he would later distill into his fiction. His restless youth in Oak Park, Illinois, led him to explore the rest of America and then move on to the still wider world overseas, an experience which would eventually serve as the source of novels and short stories alike.

But the first fictional incarnation of Hemingway's youth was the series of short stories about Nick Adams written in the twenties and thirties. Like all men, Nick Adams starts out life as an essentially innocent Adam, who nevertheless has within his personality traces of "the Old Nick," the adult who would eventually fall from grace. His two names, then, imply the fundamental struggle between good and evil which goes on in every human being as he goes through life.

Like the author of his adventures, Nick Adams grows up in Illinois, the son of a henpecked suburban doctor and an overbearing mother; he travels at home and abroad, is wounded during World War I, and returns to civilian life scarred both mentally and physically.

In Hemingway's short story cycle about young Adams, Nick is the apprentice hero who comes under the temporary influence of several code heroes, most notably Ole Andreson in "The Killers" and the Italian major in "In Another Country." Under the spell of such men Nick gradually grows in maturity from adolescence to young manhood; for it is by observing their behavior under stress that he learns how to face the harsher and more perplexing aspects of adult life.

"The Killers" has been filmed twice and a group of ten Hemingway short stories served as the basis of a movie called *Hemingway's Adventures of a Young Man*. The role of Nick Adams is slight in the first film of "The Killers" and nonexistent in the remake; but since "The Killers" as Hemingway conceived it is a Nick Adams story, I treat the two versions of the tale in concert with *Hemingway's Adventures* which share with these adaptations a common literary source.

The reason that Nick appears to be fairly expendable in the two film adaptations of "The Killers" is that in this particular short story he is not so much an actor as an observer. It is precisely the effect which witnessing the various incidents depicted in the story has on the impressionable youth that constitutes the major point of the story and binds it together thematically with the rest of the Nick Adams stories in which he is a more active participant in the action.

Admittedly Nick's role as an observer seems of relatively less importance when "The Killers" is detached from its place among the other Nick Adams stories and dramatized separately. But as Hemingway conceived it as part of his short story sequence about Nick, the tale documents the young man's first direct encounter with the forces of evil, as represented by the two paid assassins from Chicago who invade a small town to murder an ex-prizefighter called Ole Andreson. Nick is shattered by the way in which the killers have methodically gone about the business of tracking down their victim, and

Ernest Hemingway and writer-director John Huston, uncredited co-author of the script of Hemingway's favorite of all of the films based on his work, *The Killers* (1946). (Courtesy of Stuart Kaminsky)

Lily (Virginia Christine), Ole Andreson (Burt Lancaster), and Kitty Collins (Ava Gardner) in Robert Siodmak's *film noir* adaptation of *The Killers* (1946). This film established Ava Gardner as the foremost *femme fatale* of the screen for some time to come. (British Film Institute/National Film Archive)

Charlie (Lee Marvin) in the remake of *The Killers* (1964), directed by Don
Siegel. Originally intended to be the first made-for-TV movie, it was thought to
be too violent for the home screen at the time it was made and was released as
a theatrical feature instead. In contrast to the earlier version, in which the
mayhem took place mostly under cover of darkness, the brutal crimes here are
committed in broad daylight. (British Film Institute/National Film Archive)

then announce with total impunity their intent to murder Andreson in the diner where Nick is having supper.

More positively, Nick is deeply impressed by the stoic courage with which Ole accepts his unavoidable fate. After Nick warns him that the two gunmen are after him Ole continues to await their inevitable appearance in his boarding house room because, as he tells Nick, he is tired of running. "The Killers" thus represents another sobering step in Nick Adams's education in learning to cope with a cruel and disordered world. But this aspect of the story's meaning is completely passed over in both film versions of "The Killers."

Instead, each of the two motion pictures utilizes the plot of Hemingway's short story as a prologue to the film proper and then proceeds in a series of flashbacks to develop in detail the tangled web of events which lead to Ole's murder, the motive for which Hemingway never explicitly explained in the story. In effect, the two movies opt for focusing on the code hero, Ole Andreson, rather than on the apprentice hero, Nick Adams, in order to explain more fully why Ole was so willing to accept his death.

The opening sequence of the 1946 film directed by Robert Siodmak transfers Hemingway's short story to the screen virtually intact in the opening moments of the film, though even here there is a crucial departure from the original story that will be dealt with shortly. Colin McArthur writes in *Underworld USA* that Siodmak often invites his audience into the dark and sinister *film noir* world of his crime melodramas by a forward tracking shot seen from the filmgoer's point of view, and *The Killers* is no exception to this rule: "In the opening of *The Killers*, the point of view is from the back seat of the killers' car as it hurtles through the darkness towards the little town where Ole waits to be killed." [1]

The darkness which surrounds them until they enter the brightly lit diner seems to presage that during their brief stay in town the powers of darkness will hold sway. The two gunmen (William Conrad and Charles McGraw) casually announce that they plan to kill the Swede Pete Lunn (the alias which Ole Andreson has been using) when he comes in for supper. They then proceed to hold Nick, the counterman, and Sam the cook at bay. When Ole does not appear, they disappear once more into the darkness from which they had materialized a few minutes before.

Nick rushes to the boardinghouse where Ole Andreson (Burt Lancaster) lives to warn him; but it is already too late. The powers of darkness are already enveloping Ole, who lies on his bed in the murky shadows of his shabby room. He is aware that his death has only been temporarily postponed by his failure to appear in the diner for supper. After Nick departs, Ole continues to stare at the door of his room, until it suddenly bursts open and the two gunmen, minions of darkness seen only in silhouette, blast away at the camera, which then cuts to Ole's hand slowly sliding down a bedpost in death.

Aside from a few minor discrepancies, the film has up to this point been fairly faithful to its literary source. But the script omits the final scene of the short story, which takes place back at the diner, where Nick's brief conversation with George and Sam makes it clear what a traumatic experience this brush with evil has been for Nick; for his helplessness to save Ole fills him with horror and grief. It is this scene which substantiates the fact that Hemingway's short story really centers on Nick's reaction to what has happened and is not principally about Ole Andreson at all.

Asked by Gene Tunney about the real-life counterpart of Ole Andreson, Hemingway replied that it was Andre Andreson, who had agreed to throw a fight, but then went on to win it. "All afternoon he had rehearsed taking a dive," Hemingway explained; "but during the fight he had instinctively thrown a punch he didn't mean to."[2]

However, in the film Ole does not double-cross anyone by failing to throw a fight. Instead, the failure of Ole's boxing career is employed to establish Ole's desperate need for money, a need that leads him to participate in a payroll robbery with a gang that later arranges his murder for apparently double crossing them. In actual fact, we learn in a series of flashbacks, Ole is the scapegoat for Colfax, the leader of the gang (Albert Dekker), and his mistress Kitty (Ava Gardner), who use the unsuspecting Ole to cover up their own double cross of the gang. Because of his long-standing devotion to Kitty, Ole is an easy foil for their scheme. It is Kitty and Colfax who have kept the entire proceeds of the robbery for themselves while making it look like it was Ole who absconded with the funds; they leave him to take the rap and finally to be murdered once his whereabouts are discovered.

The film suggests, as does the Hemingway story, that by electing to take his medicine for consorting with criminals in the first place and by facing death with dignity and courage, Ole Andreson, the once honest boxer, redeems his recent past. Ole is, therefore, as sympathetic a figure in the film as he is in the short story, and implicitly remains the fallen code hero who regains his status in death.

As director Siodmak put it, the ideal hero for a gangster picture is someone "who has failed in life and has therefore committed a crime. . . . If you give such a person a good enough motive for the crime," the audience will be on his side. This, of course, is the recipe followed by the scriptwriters of *The Killers* and neatly sums up the way in which they have shrewdly extended Hemingway's plot to fill out a full-length screenplay.

"Scripts of the caliber of *The Killers* do not come along every day," Siodmak concluded, "This one happened to be written by my friend John Huston." [3] Huston, a distinguished writer-director in his own right of such crime melodramas as *The Maltese Falcon*, received no screen credit for collaborating on the screenplay of *The Killers* with Anthony Veiller because technically he was under contract at the time to Warner

Brothers and could not officially be credited with a screenplay for Universal.

In any event, Huston and Veiller worked well together in constructing a cleverly conceived plot. Visual continuity is supplied throughout the series of flashback sequences by a scarf decorated with golden harps which functions as a visual symbol of Ole's dedicated love of Kitty, from whom he got it as a keepsake. It first appears early in the movie in the hands of Reardan (Edmund O'Brien), the insurance investigator who has discovered it among Ole's effects after the boxer's murder. Later in the film when we see Ole fondling it during the planning session for the robbery it is an emblem of his willingness to go along with the caper in order to ingratiate himself still further with Kitty by making some easy money. Ole even wears the scarf as a mask during the actual robbery as a good luck charm. But the only kind of luck that Kitty brings Ole is bad. And it is painfully ironic, therefore, that at the time of his death this scarf embroidered with angelic harps is his sole memento of the devilish female who co-authored his murder.

The dark, shadowy atmosphere of the film epitomized in the opening sequence already described, coupled with the equally somber, cynical vision of life reflected in its tale of betrayal, disillusionment, and death, mark the film as an example of *film noir*. This trend in American cinema was in full flower when Siodmak's film was made, and the pessimistic view of life that characterized *film noir*—an outgrowth of the disillusionment spawned by World War II and its aftermath—is clearly in evidence in *The Killers*. In keeping with the conventions of the genre the film is characterized throughout by an air of grim, unvarnished realism, typified by the payroll robbery sequence. Siodmak photographed the scene with a harsh, newsreel-like quality in a single take that was as smoothly executed as the crime itself.

Hemingway himself was pleased with the movie. "The only film made from his work of which Ernest entirely approved was *The Killers*," says Mary Hemingway.[4] The studio presented him with a print of the film and he frequently ran it for guests at his home in Cuba, although he invariably fell asleep after the first reel—the only portion of the picture based directly on his story.

Undoubtedly Hemingway was happy with the $37,500 the screen rights for this single short story brought him —more than triple the sum he had received from the movie sale of his full-length novel *To Have and Have Not*. *The Killers* went on to make a handsome profit, once again giving the lie, as the movie of *For Whom the Bell Tolls* had already done, to the Hollywood superstition that movies in which the hero was killed off were also "death" at the box office.

Mark Hellinger, the producer of *The Killers*, was so elated with the picture's success that he wanted to buy four more stories from Hemingway at $75,000 a piece, plus ten percent of any profits which each of the films made beyond the one million dollar mark. Hellinger's untimely death at forty-four in 1947, however, abruptly short-circuited this arrangement. Mary Hemingway remembers that her husband returned to Hellinger's widow the check for $25,000 which he had already received from Hellinger in virtue of their new agreement.

Hemingway did not live to see the 1964 remake of *The Killers*; he would have been just as irritated at receiving no additional revenue from the remake of this short story as he was when he received nothing from the remakes of *A Farewell to Arms* and *To Have and Have Not*. In each case he had been forced to sell the screen rights of his work outright if he wanted to sell them at all. He commented stoically on this state of affairs this way in 1954: "They plan to redo *A Farewell to Arms*; I will receive nothing for it since it was sold outright. They are also about to make . . . another version of *To Have and Have Not* and maybe *The Killers*, for which they'll also pay nothing; so my hand is virtually palsied from not receiving any monies."[5]

To cash in literally and figuratively on the Hemingway

name, with great fanfare the producers of the 1964 remake of
The Killers embedded a plaque in the sidewalk in front of the
house in Oak Park, Illinois, where the author was born. The
inscription identified the house as the birthplace of the author
of their motion picture, which they had entitled *Ernest
Hemingway's The Killers*. Subsequent occupants of the house
have since removed the plaque, but the hole in the cement
where it had been is still plainly visible.

Including Hemingway's name in the title of the movie
was not only pretentious but misleading, since the remake of
The Killers, directed by Don Siegel, was considerably less
faithful to its literary source than the first version. This
demonstrated at the very outset of the Siegel film, in which
the opening sequence only remotely resembles the short
story, whereas the parallel sequence in Siodmak's movie
encapsulated most of the key elements of Hemingway's short
story.

The opening sequence in the remake is set in a home for
the blind. The peaceful atmosphere of a warm, sunny
afternoon is shattered by the chilly intrusion of two killers,
Charlie (Lee Marvin) and Lee (Clu Gulager), who have come
to murder Johnny North (John Cassavetes), a failed auto racer
who teaches a course in auto repair to the blind inmates of the
home. A blind old man (instead of young Nick Adams) warns
Johnny that two sinister strangers are looking for him; but
Johnny does not flee. Instead, he resolutely stands his ground
as the two assailants burst into his classroom and fill him with
lead.

Charlie and Lee are impressed by the tranquility with
which Johnny North has met his fate, and they resolve to find
out why, particularly because Charlie remembers that four
years before, North was implicated in a million dollar mail
truck heist from which the stolen money was never recovered.

From this point onward the new "adaptation" proceeds in
flashback fashion, the same format used in the previous movie
to fill in the background behind the hero's death. This time

the femme fatale who suckers the hero into getting involved in a robbery is Sheila Farr (Angie Dickinson). Like Kitty, her predecessor in the first movie, she then manages to con the rest of the gang into believing that Johnny has double-crossed them and made off with all of the plunder, when in fact it is Sheila and her lover, Jack Browning (Ronald Reagan), who have done the double crossing.

After strong-arming several people who knew Johnny for information about his past, Charlie and Lee decide to blackmail Browning by threatening to tell the mob that it is he and Sheila who should have been murdered. Browning ambushes the two blackmailers from his office window, killing Lee instantly and mortally wounding Charlie. But Charlie lives long enough to dispatch both Browning and Sheila after cornering them in Browning's fashionable home.

As he draws a bead on them, Sheila begs him to listen to her spurious excuses for her part in the whole affair. Before firing, Charlie shakes his head wearily and murmurs for the last time in the film his oft-repeated remark, "I just haven't got the time." The middle-aged Charlie has known along that given the many years he has already survived the perils of his profession as a paid assassin he is living on borrowed time; he is now aware that his time has at last run out.

After he shoots Browning and Sheila, Charlie staggers out of the house into the bright sunlight and collapses. Hearing a police siren in the distance, he raises his arm, points his index finger as if it were his revolver, and dies. Charlie knows his arsenal is exhausted, just as he knows his life is spent; but he nevertheless makes this one final futile gesture of defiance against the forces of law and order as he expires and the movie ends.

Though the remake of *The Killers* has little connection with Hemingway, it is an excellent thriller in itself. Siegel —whom Hellinger had wanted to direct the original adaptation of the story—and scriptwriter Gene Coon sought to avoid making a mere rehash of the Siodmak film by introducing some neat plot twists of their own, such as having the killers themselves, rather than an insurance investigator, probe the motives for the hero's steadfast refusal to avoid his own murder.

Even the look of Siegel's film is different from that of Siodmak's movie. Since Siodmak shot his film in black and white and Siegel's movie was to be in color, the latter decided to replace the ominously dark atmosphere of Siodmak's *film noir* with several scenes of mayhem shot in bright sunshine to imply that in the savage world of the film, evil is just as likely to strike in broad daylight as under the cover of darkness.

Although Siegel's film was designed to be the first made-for-TV movie ever done, Siegel has told me that he did not shoot the picture any differently because of that: "I shot it the way I shoot every film I make, in a very taut, lean style with great economy, and at a very fast pace. This is the way I work best."

Yet shooting had gotten off to a bad start when Lee Marvin took to showing up on the set in no condition to work, and Siegel became increasingly worried that Marvin's drinking was hurting the picture. The crucial final scene of the film had been shot on the first day of production on location in a posh suburban home which the studio had rented for the day. But it had to be reshot later because Marvin had arrived drunk, and redoing the scene, of course, meant an expensive return to the location site.

When similar incidents occurred, Siegel finally decided to take the actor aside during a break in shooting and tell Marvin of his concern: "Look, you just can't work when you're like this," Siegel said. "I could shoot it and use it, but you'd look bad. So let's go through it one more time for show, call it a day, and do it right tomorrow." Later in the day Marvin remarked to Siegel: "I liked the fact that you talked to me alone." From then on, adds Siegel, Marvin did not show up drunk for the duration of shooting.

Siegel elicited from Marvin the best performance of his

career as a psychotic killer who dresses impeccably and carries his revolver in a businesslike attaché case emblematic of his cool professionalism. In another fortuituous bit of casting Siegel cast Ronald Reagan against type as the villain of the piece in what turned out to be, interestingly enough, the actor's last film before launching a career in politics. "There *is* something ironic," says Siegel wryly, "about the man who was to become the governor of California executing the robbery of a mail truck in the movie disguised as a California state trooper." Quite apart from this curious sidelight on Reagan's farewell performance in the film, he gave a fine, sharp-edged performance as Browning.

Although Siegel shoots a film with economy and speed, he takes his time in the editing room, where he and editor Richard Belding spent twenty-five days working round the clock to turn the 180,000 feet of the rough cut of *The Killers* into a final print of 9,000 feet, so that the film would fit into a two-hour TV time slot.[6]

As things turned out the movie was first released as a theatrical feature and not premiered on television after all. The sponsors thought the film too violent for the home screen and NBC concurred, especially since the recent assassination of President Kennedy had sparked protests from the public about TV violence promoting violence in real life. Moreover, the scene in which Browning ambushes Charlie and Lee from a vantage point high above the street was thought to resemble the circumstances of the President's death too closely, although the similarity was purely coincidental. The picture achieved a successful theatrical release which confirmed Siegel's position as a preeminent director of fast-paced thrillers, although it does not quite come up to Siodmak's classic *film noir* version of the Hemingway story. For one thing, whatever the movie's other merits, the Siegel film had little to do with the original short story and nothing at all to do with Nick Adams—and the producers' ploy of including Hemingway's name in the official title of the film could not conceal that fact. Indeed, Siegel wanted the film simply called *Johnny North*, but was overruled by the front office.

Two years earlier Martin Ritt had made a film which also employed Hemingway's name in the title, and which brought to the screen several of the Nick Adams stories. It was entitled *Hemingway's Adventures of a Young Man*, although its working title had simply been *Young Man*. The script for this 1962 film was by Aaron Hotchner, whose TV adaptations of Hemingway's fiction, including some of the Nick Adams stories, had for the most part pleased Hemingway.

The first of the Nick Adams stories which Hotchner had adapted for TV had been "The Battler," which was telecast in October 1955 as part of NBC's *Playwright's '56* series and directed by Arthur Penn. A young Broadway actor named Paul Newman was to play Nick, and James Dean had been cast as Ad Francis, the punchy prizefighter of the title, whom Hemingway had based on Ad Wolgast, a former lightweight champion who ended his days shadowboxing in a padded cell. On September 30, 1955, two days before rehearsals were to begin, however, Dean was killed in a sportscar accident and Newman was hastily pressed into service to play the battler. Newman brought off his characterization of the battered pug perfectly, and would recreate the role of Ad Francis nearly a decade later in the Nick Adams motion picture.

The success of "The Battler" on the tube warranted a dramatization of seven of the Nick Adams stories on the CBS program called *The Seven Lively Arts* in 1957 under the collective title *The World of Nick Adams*, which was directed by Robert Mulligan and scored by Aaron Copland. Hemingway was again satisfied with Hotchner's work as an adapter of his fiction; and he himself suggested three years later that Hotchner turn the teleplay into a full-scale movie script, which would draw on three additional Hemingway short stories.

Twentieth Century-Fox responded to Hotchner's query about the project through Jerry Wald, the producer of *The*

Breaking Point, with an offer of $100,000 for the screen rights to the ten stories. Hotchner thought this a reasonable sum, but Hemingway did not. At this point in Hemingway's life, the latter's physical and mental health were steadily declining and he was only a year away from his tragic suicide. He was inordinately worried about rising taxes and declining royalties, though his wife and business advisers had repeatedly assured him about his firm financial status. Nevertheless Hemingway felt compelled to hold out for nine times the amount that Fox had offered him for the stories, pointing out that the same company had paid $75,000 for his short story "The Snows of Kilimanjaro" alone.

Hotchner tactfully defended Fox's offer, however, reminding Hemingway that several of the stories in the package had already been seen in the not-too-distant past on national television and that Fox was paying for the rights to do only a single motion picture based on all ten stories, not one film per story. Fox's final bid was $125,000 which Hemingway finally but grudgingly accepted. With that, Hotchner went to work on the script.

In discussing the design of the screenplay with Hemingway only a few months before the novelist's death, Hotchner learned that Hemingway was concerned lest the public assume that the film was really a thinly disguised autobiography. "Nick Adams bears the same relation to my boyhood," he explained, "as Huck Finn to Mark Twain's boyhood."[7] In other words, while there are undeniable parallels between Nick's youthful experiences and those of his creator, the Nick Adams stories are not mere snippets of personal autobiography. Hemingway's creative imagination developed the autobiographical elements on which the various stories were founded into fully realized works of fiction that range far beyond the initial real-life incidents which may have triggered them.

For example, Hemingway had never witnessed his father delivering a baby under harrowing circumstances as Nick does in the story "Indian Camp." But he did as a lad once happen upon a woman in the throws of labor at the side of a road, and he did what he could to help her; and that incident served as the genesis of "Indian Camp." Consequently although there would be definite analogies between Hemingway's life and Nick Adam's adventures in the movie, it is Nick's story and not Hemingway's that Hotchner set out to narrate in his screenplay.

Pauline Kael is incorrect when she accuses the makers of the Nick Adams movie of slyly combining Hemingway's fiction with incidents from his life and serving up the results "as some sort of biographical film about Ernest Hemingway."[8] The similarities between Nick Adams and Ernest Hemingway to be found in the film are essentially those which preexisted in the fiction.

Some of Nick's experiences likewise prefigure those of later Hemingway apprentice heroes because, as I noted earlier, Nick Adams is the fundamental apprentice hero in Hemingway's fiction, on whom all of the subsequent key apprentice heroes in Hemingway's work are based. As Philip Young puts it, the experiences of childhood, adolescence, and young manhood which shaped Nick Adams also shaped Frederic Henry, Robert Jordan, and other apprentice heroes in Hemingway's later fiction. "They have all had Nick's childhood, Nick's adolescence, Nick's young manhood."[9]

Because the protagonists of Hemingway's fiction are, in Hotchner's phrase, "blood relatives" of each other, the scriptwriter was quite justified in drawing on the experiences of later Hemingway heroes to flesh out the full-length portrait of Nick Adams in his screenplay. For example, if Hemingway himself developed *A Farewell to Arms* from material contained seminally in the Nick Adams stories, it seems both artistically and dramatically right that Hotchner should utilize details from that novel to fill in the gaps in the sketchy treatment of Nick's war experiences as they are found in the short story sequence.

"The stories are connected only by the fact that Nick

appears in all of them; other than that they are isolated experiences of fear, disillusionment, courage, love, war, and loneliness," Hotchner points out, and not chapters in a continuing narrative. "But to fuse them and embellish them for the screen without disturbing their impact, was a particularly difficult assignment."[10] To carry out his task Hotchner selected from the ten short stories he was using those incidents which would best hang together as an ongoing narrative and then created additional material, sometimes with the aid of Hemingway's other fiction, to link each episode with the next and to give it added depth and detail.

To establish the theme of the film as the growth of a young man from youth to maturity, a narrator (whose delivery is obviously meant to approximate Hemingway's own voice) tells us: "In the place where you are born and grow up you begin to know the things that all men must know. Although they are the simplest things, it takes a man's life really to know them."

With that the film launches into the first of the Nick Adams stories used in the screenplay, "The Doctor and the Doctor's Wife," in which Nick (Richard Beymer) is ashamed to watch his father (Arthur Kennedy) being intimidated by a half-breed handyman in much the same way that Dr. Adams allows his wife (Jessica Tandy) to dominate him in the scene that follows. (Hemingway said of this story that his own hatred for his mother was "non-Freudian," that she was "an all-time bitch," and that the first psychic wound of his life had been occasioned by his discovery as a lad that his father was a coward.[11])

This negative picture of Nick's father is to some degree balanced, however, by the way he appears in "Indian Camp," and the story is employed for the same purpose in the film. Nick accompanies his father to the nearby Indian camp and observes him in his professional capacity as a doctor performing an emergency cesarean section without benefit of anesthetic for the Indian mother or proper surgical instruments for the operation.

To reinforce the contrast between the way in which Nick sees his father in these two complementary episodes, the screenplay makes the arrogant half-breed the father of the baby whom Dr. Adams is delivering. The man who had insulted the doctor earlier cannot bear to watch the operation and runs from the cabin to escape witnessing the ordeal. In Hemingway's story the father of the baby actually slits his own throat when he can no longer stand the anguished screams of his wife as she suffers an arduous and prolonged labor without any pain killer. The suicide is omitted in the movie, however, thereby severely undercutting the impact of the original story, which reflects Nick's initiation into the pain and violence often associated with both birth and death.

The impact of the incidents of "Indian Camp" on Nick is further softened in the motion picture treatment of the tale, however, because Nick is not a small boy, as he is in the short story, but a lad in his late teens, as he is throughout the film. In the short story, then, the events which Nick witnesses make a much greater impression on him than they do on the older Nick of the movie. (In addition, as Philip Young notes, "Indian Camp" as Hemingway wrote it sets the pattern for Nick's later contacts with violence and evil, culminating in his own wound in World War I.)

Presumably the script raises Nick's age to eighteen or so from the very beginning of the film and does not allow him to grow from childhood into his teens as he does in the short story sequence, in order to glide more easily into the material dealing with his adolescent experiences on the road. Nick's increasing unhappiness with his home situation finally stimulates him to leave his family behind and set out to see the world beyond the insulated atmosphere of his home town. In the course of his peregrinations he encounters the ruined ex-boxing champion Ad Francis (Paul Newman) and his black traveling companion, Bugs (Juano Hernandez), of the story "The Battler." Joining them at their campfire, Nick tells them of the beating he received from a sadistic brake-man on a freight train. Later, Ad suddenly becomes hostile to Nick in a similar manner, but this time Bugs saves Nick from further injury by administering a love tap with a blackjack on the back of Ad's head. Bugs tactfully tells Nick that he had better move on; as Nick takes his leave, Bugs is cradling Ad in his lap and gently nursing the permanently punch-drunk fighter back to consciousness.

Young calls "The Battler" as unpleasant as anything that Hemingway ever wrote; and the dark implications of sado-masochism exhibited in the relationship of Ad and Bugs are not lost on Nick in the story or in the film, as he walks into the night stunned by his first exposure to a brand of human behavior which he has never encountered before. Nick, one infers, will not have to wait until he gets to the battlefield to experience physical violence and psychic pain.

When he does reach the Italian front as an ambulance driver, Nick is wounded and falls in love with a nurse while he is recuperating in a military hospital, just as he does in "A Very Short Story."[12] This two-page story is very short indeed and served as the fundamental material which Hemingway elaborated into *A Farewell to Arms*. The screenplay according-ly develops the love relationship of Nick and his girl along the lines of that of Frederick Henry and Catherine Barkley in what amounts to a distillation of the love story of *Farewell*— except that Nick's beloved is killed in an air raid instead of dying in childbirth as Catherine does. But the upshot of the romance is the same in both cases: the hero loses the first person to whom he has been able to commit himself in a lasting love relationship and is left desolate and sobered by his experiences of love and war.

In the war episodes of the short story sequence, Heming-way provides Nick with a code hero to whom he can look for emotional support and inspiration in a way that he could not look to earlier failed code heroes like his father. This code hero is the Italian major whom Nick comes to know in the story entitled "In Another Country," and who implicitly fulfills the same function of father figure/code hero in the film as well. The major (Ricardo Montalban), a former fencing champion whose hand has been crushed in battle, will never fence again; he is admirable in the way that he sustains this and other cruel blows of fate with stoic equanimity, and he encourages Nick to do the same.

The harsh experiences with which Nick has met in the course of his travels in both peace and war leave their mark on him, and he returns home at the end of the movie crippled in both mind and body. Here he is met by the news that his father committed suicide while he was gone. The circumstances of Dr. Adams's death are only vaguely suggested in the story "Fathers and Sons," but the film fills out the details by borrowing what Robert Jordan says about his father's death in *For Whom the Bell Tolls*: that his father's suicide proved that he had always been a coward. "Because if he wasn't a coward he would have stood up to that woman and not let her bully him."[13]

In the light of what has previously been noted about all of Hemingway's major protagonists, including Robert Jordan, sharing Nick's early history as their own, it seems quite legitimate for the movie to explain the death of Nick's father more fully by making reference to *For Whom the Bell Tolls*. In sum, if Hemingway could draw on the Nick Adams stories in writing his later fiction, it only seems fair that Hotchner could draw on the later fiction when supplying needed details for his screenplay of the Nick Adams stories. The adaptor is only taking advantage of the continuity in Hemingway's fiction which the writer himself had already put there.

Nick finally realizes that he will have to leave home for good if he is to escape the continued dominance of his mother and to profit by the hard-earned maturity which he has gained in the recent past. As Nick stands on the lake shore, suitcase in hand, and looks toward the horizon and his future, the narrator's voice returns: "For the last time you look at the lake at the side of the house where you were born. Tomorrow you will try again, but this time you're not running away; you're running toward something. . . ."

Despite the author's lifelong fear of the microphone, producer Jerry Wald had hoped to get Hemingway to record the narration that begins and ends the film; however, by the time the film went into production Hemingway had, like the father of Nick Adams, and the father of Robert Jordan, and his own father, ended his life by his own hand. Hotchner, along with Wald and director Martin Ritt, were scouting locations for the movie in Europe when they got this news in July 1961. Hotchner was reminded of his last phone conversation with Hemingway a few weeks earlier, in which, after inquiring about the script, Hemingway advised: "Well, Hotch, don't forget that old Cherokee saying—you pays your money and you takes your chances. Just don't play it safe." Then Hemingway concluded: "Even if it doesn't work, you're all right. The hell with playing it safe."[14]

According to Hotchner's interview with Frank Laurence, it was producer Jerry Wald, and not he, who wanted the script "to play it safe" and avoid running the risk of offending the mass audience in any way. If so, Wald's attitude hardly coincides with his assertion that the filmmaker's prime responsibility in adapting a literary property to the screen centers on his respect for "the intent, the flavor, the theme, and the spirit of the original."

At Wald's behest, for example, the suicide of the Indian husband in "Indian Camp" was cut from the finished screenplay of the film because he was worried that since the picture was to end with the revelation of Dr. Adams's suicide another suicide in the film might prove offensive to audiences. If Wald did not heed Hemingway's advice not to play it safe, at least he followed the novelist's suggestion that for the war segments in the film the moviemakers "use Verona and the countryside around Caprino, where Nick Adams fought his war and was wounded."

The film unit was often plagued by bad weather and overcast skies throughout the shooting period in Italy, but director Ritt and his cinematographer, Lee Garmes, at times were able to use the prevailing dim light to good advantage. A love scene between Nick and Rosanna, the nurse with whom he has fallen in love, was shot in an ancient courtyard filled with massive statues. According to journalist Herb Lightman, Ritt decided to create an atmosphere of impending doom by photographing "the monolithic forms in somber light from angles that made them seem to threaten the ill-fated soldier and nurse walking in the courtyard below."[15]

A sense of foreboding also surrounds the scene in which candles waver precariously before the statue of St. Anthony in the church that has been converted into a temporary hospital, as Rosanna "presents" Nick to her favorite saint. Later, as Rosanna lies dying in the same hospital-church, the candles in front of St. Anthony's shrine have been extinguished, a rueful premonition that her life is soon to be snuffed out as well.

There are some other finely wrought visual symbols in the movie. For example, when Dr. Adams is summoned by his wife to her room near the beginning of the film, he is photographed through the bannister bars as he climbs the stairs, indicating how his submission to her stronger will imprisons his spirit. Inside the room his wife sits in semidarkness; even after Dr. Adams raises the shades the shadowy atmosphere persists to cast a sense of gloom over their relationship.

Darkness is used differently but just as effectively in the scene in which Nick meets Ad Francis for the first time. Ad is barely visible as he sits some distance from the flickering light of the campfire. We soon learn, as Nick does, that Ad inhabits a murky fantasy world of his own concoction, in which he is still the iron-constitutioned champion against whose body hapless contenders could only "bust their hands."[16] Ad sits in shadows because his pathetic delusions cannot withstand even the light of a campfire, much less the light of day.

Despite the credentials and expertise of its veteran director, writer, and cinematographer, *Hemingway's Adventures of a Young Man* remains a motion picture of uneven quality. The principal blame for this must be shouldered by its star, Richard Beymer, a handsome young actor who simply lacked the range which the part required. He was chosen by Wald because at the time Fox was grooming Beymer to be a superstar. Unfortunately, he had not yet developed a strong enough screen presence to hold his own opposite old pros like Arthur Kennedy and Jessica Tandy, much less the array of formidable talents—Paul Newman heads the list—who turned up throughout the movie in cameo roles and who constantly overshadowed Beymer's pallid portrayal of Nick.

Moreover, although the overriding theme of the film, Nick's progress from youth to young manhood, permeates the screenplay, it is not reflected in Beymer's portrayal of Nick. The young actor does not build a consistent performance which reflects Nick's gradual growth toward maturity. The only difference between Beymer's performance at the beginning and at the end of the film, one critic pointed out, is that by the movie's conclusion he walks with a limp. The comment is flippant, but not altogether unfair. In fact, Beymer was so discouraged by the consistently poor notices which he received for this film and others that he dropped out of films altogether not long after.

Although certainly not a great motion picture, *Hemingway's Adventures of a Young Man* has its moments, and it is surely not the "disgrace" that Pauline Kael deemed it.

In the next chapter I shall continue to examine the treatment of Hemingway's short stories on the screen with a consideration of *The Macomber Affair* and *Under My Skin*. As in the case of the two versions of *The Killers* examined here, we shall once more be made aware of the perils involved in extending short stories into full-length feature films.

6
Short Unhappy Lives:
The Macomber Affair (1947) and *Under My Skin* (1950)

A.E. HOTCHNER DESCRIBES THE TASK OF adapting a work of fiction to the screen as a perilous high-wire act. Adaptation by its very nature, he explains, forces the scriptwriter "to deal with people not his own, set against backgrounds not of his invention. With varying degrees of success the adapter tries to identify with these people, but he does not often succeed, for it is like adopting a full-grown orphan." In expanding a short story into a full-length film, Hotchner continues, the scriptwriter must so compose the invented scenes that they will preserve the spirit of the material which inspired them, avoiding the creation of any situation or character which seems out of keeping with the tone and style of the original author's work.[1] "A screenwriter is at best a stylistic chameleon," adds Philip Dunne; "he writes in the style of the original source—or should, if he's worth his salt."[2]

In the case of *The Macomber Affair* (1947), the original source was Hemingway's brilliant 1936 short story, "The

Short Happy Life of Francis Macomber," which he wrote after his return from the African safari described in *The Green Hills of Africa* (1935). Its companion story, "The Snows of Kilimanjaro," also owes its inception to this same 1934 safari; and the creative spark which fired Hemingway's imagination to compose both stories was kindled by Philip Percival, the sagacious guide who accompanied him on the trip.

In the evenings by the campfire Percival would often regale Hemingway over whiskey and soda with bits of African lore and with reminiscences of his previous safaris. Several of the latter tales centered on the growth in courage of inexperienced hunters. Hemingway decided to tell the story of one such young hunter and call him Francis Macomber. Of Macomber's wife, Margaret, Hemingway later said: "I invented her complete with handles from the worst bitch I knew, and when I first knew her she'd been lovely."[3]

Robert Wilson, the courageous white hunter of the story, was shaped from the personality of Percival himself. To these ingredients Hemingway added his own personal knowledge and experience of big game hunting and fashioned the story of how Francis at first disgraces himself by fleeing from a charging lion but subsequently redeems himself the following day by bagging a ferocious buffalo. The tale ends with Margaret shooting her husband accidentally-on-purpose because she realizes that his new-found courage and restored self-esteem will preclude her dominating him in the future as she had done in the past. Margaret thus represents what Edmund Wilson has styled the genuine American bitch: "the impossible civilized woman who despises the civilized man for his failure in initiative and nerve," and then jealously seeks to destroy him when he begins to exhibit these qualities.[4]

Francis Macomber is the apprentice hero of the story who learns under the tutelage of Wilson, the code hero, the principle that "in the ethics of shooting dangerous game," as Hemingway puts it, "the trouble you shoot yourself into you must be prepared to shoot yourself out of."[5] Because in principle physical courage implies moral courage, this mandate, of course, means that man must learn to stand fast in the face of adversity wherever he encounters it; and by embracing this principle Francis has *ipso facto* taken a lease on a new life. Ironically he does not realize that he is being stalked by the predatory Margaret even while he is stalking the buffalo; and she abruptly fells her prey immediately after he fells his, thus ending the all-too-brief new life of Francis Macomber.

The movie rights of "The Short Happy Life" were purchased for $75,000 by veteran screenwriter Casey Robinson, who was to act as co-writer and co-producer for the present film, for the 1950 *Under My Skin* (based on "My Old Man"), and *The Snows of Kilimanjaro* (1952). As both producer and scriptwriter, Robinson had much more of a say in the way that his screenplays for these stories were converted into motion pictures and therefore perhaps deserves a larger share of whatever praise or blame accrues to these films than anyone else associated with them.

Robinson decided to take his *Macomber* script to independent producer Benedict Bogeaus rather than to one of the large studios, in which the front office would impose far more supervision on the making of the movie. "I try, when I'm writing a screenplay from somebody's original work," he explained, "to be as faithful to it as I can be, within the limitations of a screenplay and remembering that the novel medium and the screen are entirely different."[6] There is widespread critical agreement that, except for the film's ending, *The Macomber Affair* is as close as any movie has yet come to reproducing Hemingway on the screen.

In the film, the central plot of the short story is told in one extended flashback sandwiched between a prologue and an epilogue set in the present. The picture begins with a plane materializing out of the darkness of an African airfield as Wilson (Gregory Peck) and Margaret Macomber (Joan Bennett) return from the jungle with the corpse of her husband, Francis (Robert Preston). Wilson and Margaret are met by a

Margaret Macomber (Joan Bennett) and Robert Wilson (Gregory Peck) in the screen version of "The Short Happy Life of Francis Macomber," entitled *The Macomber Affair* (1947). This film is generally agreed to be one of the most faithful versions of a Hemingway story ever filmed, except for its softened ending. (The Museum of Modern Art/Film Stills Archive)

police detective charged with investigating Francis's death; the fog that swirls around them as he questions them serves as an apt metaphor for the mystery which as yet surrounds the demise of Francis Macomber.

As Wilson fills out a report for the police in his hotel room, the movie shifts into flashback and portrays the events leading up to the fatal shooting. The only significant departure which the movie makes from its literary source during the long flashback which comprises the central section of the film is to imply that Wilson has fallen in love with Margaret. This introduces an element of conventional movie romance which is wholly absent from Hemingway's story. It is true that Margaret goes to Wilson's tent during the night following Francis's debacle with the lion in both the short story and the film; but it is evident in Hemingway's version that their adulterous tryst is a mutual gesture of contempt for Francis's unmanly display of cowardliness and not even partially motivated by anything like ripening love.

Otherwise the film adaptation proceeds in a manner that is fairly close to the original story, up to and including the point near the end of the film at which Wilson coldly accuses Margaret of liquidating her husband because, after his African adventure, Francis would no longer be as passive and pliable a mate as he had been in the past. At this point, however, the movie abruptly swerves from the short story by having Wilson immediately retract what he has just said, with the explanation that he was only testing her to see if she could stand up under similar questioning at the inquest.

The dialogue of the film, which throughout the movie had very often been taken verbatim from the story, now leaves Hemingway behind in order to swing the audience's sympathies away from the dead Francis to Margaret by means of her very sincerely expressed doubts about her culpability in shooting her husband, and by her account of how Francis had really forced her into becoming the kind of tough female that she has exhibited herself to be as her sole means of defense against his slyly manipulative behavior. "I thought I could change him but he changed me," she says. "I knew he was weak, and finally I gave up and became bitter. I could feel his rottenness spreading through me, but by then I didn't care." She concludes: "I saw him in the gun sight, but I saw the buffalo too. Maybe I killed him. If there is such a thing as murder in the heart, there is your answer."

As the film would have it, Margaret has experienced a genuine change of heart; for she has firmly and finally decided to tell her story at the inquest as honestly as she has just related it to Wilson. With his encouragement shoring her up, Margaret resolutely turns toward the courtroom where she is to testify, now secure in her conviction that she is better off risking prison by telling the truth as she understands it than in living with her unresolved doubts.

Margaret in the movie is thus presented as a long-suffering woman who undoubtedly deserves to be exonerated by the official inquiry, as Wilson has assured her that she will be, once she has expiated whatever subconscious responsibility that she may have for her husband's death by willingly and honestly facing the ordeal of the hearing.

This attempt in the movie's final moments to retool Margaret into a more sympathetic character follows from the fact that the film had already established that Margaret and Wilson had fallen in love. Accordingly the moviemakers wanted to present Margaret as a worthy romantic screen heroine who deserved to be reunited with her screen lover, Wilson, once the odious matter of Francis's death has been settled. But as Hemingway told the story, there is no love lost between Margaret and Wilson. Their mutual attraction is purely sexual, and as such is short-lived.

Margaret's change of heart was also dictated by the prevailing film morality standards of the time, according to which the makers of *The Macomber Affair* feared that audience sensibilities might be offended by a vicious wife coolly dispatching her unwanted husband and thus getting away with murder. In the short story, however, Margaret will still have to go on living with her guilt and with the fact that Wilson's knowledge of the crime has given him the upper hand over her; he can therefore take advantage of her if he cares too. And the odds are, moreover, that he will do so since, as Arthur Waldhorn writes in commenting on the short story, Wilson is "an admitted opportunist in everything but the hunting."[7] Margaret's nasty situation at the end of the short story should therefore have been precarious and unpleasant enough to satisfy movie morality.

It is a pity, consequently, that Robinson and his collaborators saw fit to compromise the ending by imposing a spurious love story on Hemingway's material and in the last reel realigning Margaret's character in a futile attempt to make her a more sympathetic romantic heroine. Precisely because the screenplay has been faithful to the story in presenting Margaret as a calloused and calculating woman throughout the film, however, her eleventh-hour change of heart in the closing moments of the movie seems too abrupt and inconsistent with her established personality, and therefore hardly credible.

In any event, *The Macomber Affair* was not a popular film, though it deserves to be seen for many of the splendid elements which it contains. One of the best moments in the film is the scene in which we see Francis in his tent rolling and tossing in fitful sleep on the night following his cowardly behavior on the hunt. Superimposed on his sleeping figure is a shot of Wilson and Margaret kissing in Wilson's tent, followed by a shot of an onrushing lion. Then Francis awakens, as he does in the short story, to find Margaret's cot unoccupied, signifying that his dream of her infidelity is a reality. In this brief but brilliant montage sequence the connection is made visually between Francis's cowardice and Margaret's disappearance into Wilson's tent by associating the image of the lion both with Wilson's virility and with Francis's unmanly lack of courage. The montage further implies that Francis's virile demonstration of courage on the morrow will at least be partially spurred on by his jealous anger.

The film's director, Zoltan Korda, had an uneven career in pictures, but *The Macomber Affair* is surely his best film. The quality of the movie was helped immeasurably by the brooding musical score contributed by Miklos Rosza and by the cinematography of Karl Struss, one of Hollywood's best cameramen, who had worked with Griffith, Chaplin, and DeMille. For *The Macomber Affair*, Struss recalled, "We re-created Africa in Mexico," though several critics assumed that the film's authentic look meant that it was actually shot entirely on location in Africa.

Struss had little respect for Korda, calling the director "a phoney" who needlessly reshot scenes, apparently to impress cast and crew alike with his thoroughness and insistence on perfection. "We shot all day in one place," Struss said, "and suddenly that night Korda almost casually announced to Peck and the others that he would do the whole thing all over again the next day. It was completely pointless, and the second day's shooting was exactly the same as the first, except for some tiny gesture of Greg's."[8]

Nevertheless, under Korda's direction Gregory Peck, Robert Preston, and Joan Bennett turned in a trio of uniformly good performances. As film critic Robert Morsberger sums it up, "Peck's laconic performance conveyed a sense of self-control by contrast to Preston's boyish eagerness and emotional messiness. As Margaret, Joan Bennett was beautifully bitchy, in perhaps the best performance of her career. But Preston had the richest role and received superlative reviews."[9]

It is unfortunate that Hemingway should have chosen to deride a movie that was by and large a serious and faithful rendition of his short story. Hemingway claimed that producer Darryl F. Zanuck, whom he at times referred to as "Darryl F. Panic," called him about choosing a title for the film while he, Hemingway, was vacationing in Sun Valley. The novelist was advised that the studio felt that the title of the original story was too long to fit on a movie marquee, and he was asked to supply a shorter title that would appeal to both sexes. The novelist said that he left Zanuck waiting on the other end of the long-distance line for several expensive minutes while he came up with the following suggested title: "F as in Fox, U as in Universal, C as in Culver City, and K as in RKO. That should fit all the marquees, and you can't beat it as a sex symbol."[10] The authenticity of this story is dubious, if for no other reason than that as an executive at Fox, Zanuck had absolutely nothing to do with the making of *The Macomber Affair*, which was made independently by Benedict Bogeaus for United Artists release.

One of the things that led Robinson to collaborate on a film of "The Short Happy Life" was its theme of how a man grows in maturity by accepting the challenges of life, as Francis finally does on the buffalo hunt. Robinson had expressed this concept explicitly in his script for *King's Row* (1941). "The idea that some people just grow old while other people grow up," as he puts it, was at the heart of *King's Row*.[11] It was also implicit in *The Macomber Affair* in the person of Francis Macomber and in the next Hemingway film that Robinson wrote and produced, *Under My Skin* (1950), based on another Hemingway short story, "My Old Man."

"The Short Happy Life of Francis Macomber" is a fairly long short story by Hemingway standards, and it included sufficient plot complications to be developed into a full-length screenplay without much additional material. "My Old Man," on the other hand, is a simpler tale, only half the length of "Macomber," and its plot therefore required considerably more elaboration if it was to be made into a feature-length film.

One of Hemingway's earliest published stories, it was based on his observations of what he had seen and heard at the racetracks he had frequented while he was in Europe during World War I, and when he returned there in the postwar years. It is not, therefore, the true story of any single jockey. "You had to digest life and create your own people," he wrote in a short piece entitled "On Writing," and he cites "My Old Man" as an example of what he means. Though the jockey in his story dies during a race, Hemingway had never witnessed such a death at the track before composing the story. Yet the week after he finished the story "Georges Parfrement was killed at that very jump and that was the way it looked."[12] "My Old Man" does indeed exude the authentic flavor of the racetrack and was promptly printed in *The Best Short Stories of 1923* after Hemingway showed it to the editor of the anthology, Edward O'Brien, who liked it so much that he dedicated the whole volume to the neophyte writer.

The story is narrated by Joe Butler, the young son of a jockey, who idolizes his "old man." The lad sometimes observes his father's shady dealings with gamblers around the track, but never grasps the grim import of his father's behavior. It seems in one scene that Joe's dad has failed to throw a race that he had agreed to lose, just as Ole Andreson in "The Killers" apparently had not taken a dive in a fight which he had agreed to lose. As Joe watches a couple of menacing types berate his father after the race, he is sickened by the fact that anybody "could call my old man a son-of-a-bitch and get away with it." Afterward his father tries to pass over the matter by saying: "You got to take a lot of things in this world, Joe."

Clearly Joe is the apprentice hero of the story, one of the youngest that Hemingway ever depicted, and his father is one of Hemingway's more tarnished code heroes, a man who has gradually compromised his principles of sportsmanship over the years by getting involved with racetrack gamblers. Yet in the scene just described Joe's old man does try to give the boy an example of the kind of endurance which the lad will need in order to stand up to whatever life has in store for him. Joe's father even tries to make a comeback as an honest jockey for the sake of his son. But, aging and out of condition as he is, he no longer has what it takes even to finish a race, and he dies in a muddy pileup of horses and riders.

The final twist of the story is Joe's overhearing two track regulars commenting on his father's death as his just deserts for his crooked finagling of the past. George Gardner, another jockey, urges Joe to disregard what he has overheard; but the heartbroken boy can only say: "Seems like when they get started they don't leave a guy nothing."[13] Not only has Joe's father been taken away from him in death but his idealized picture of his dad has been shattered beyond repair, leaving the boy with an even nothing.

When Casey Robinson bought "My Old Man" for $45,000 on behalf of Twentieth Century-Fox to write and produce a film derived from it, he did not have much more plot material to work with than I have just outlined above. The relationship between Joe and his old man as son (apprentice hero) and father (code hero) is for all practical purposes carried over into the movie, but Robinson had to add a considerable number of complications to the plot in order to stretch the story into a feature motion picture. Unfortunately he accomplished this task not wisely but too well, for the convoluted twists and turns of the movie's story line are sometimes hard to follow—particularly when casual references are made in the dialogue to past events that are never fully explained in the course of the movie. The screenplay has jockey Dan Butler (John Garfield) falling in love with a character not in the short story, a French girl name Paule (Micheline Presle), who has taken a liking to his son, Joe (Oley Lindgren); but Paule initially despises Dan for being a crooked jockey. Joe's devotion to both of them eventually brings them together, but Paule is right about Dan's dirty dealings at the track.

Dan desperately promises gambler Louis Bork (Luther Adler) to throw a race in order to pay off his debts to the mobster; but in the grand finale of the film he decides to try to win the race anyhow to make Joe proud of him. Dan dies in the film, but only after he has ridden to victory, not before the race is finished as in the short story.

The rest of the movie departs even more substantially from Hemingway's story. Joe does not learn the full scope of his father's past duplicity after Dan's death, as he does in the short story. Instead George Gardner speaks an encomium for Dan in which he assures the boy that Dan's name deserves to be added to the track's honor roll of jockeys. "Sure," replies Joe in the movie's last line, "he was my old man." With that Joe and Paule walk away from the camera together; Joe's admiration of his dead father is still intact and he has someone with whom he can share his life (and the prize money of his father's last race).

John Garfield's hard-nosed portrayal of Dan all but rescued the movie from the sentimentality of the adaptation, epitomized in the sugar-coated ending. At this late period in his career (he would himself be dead in two years) Garfield had reached the peak of his powers as an actor, as he proved here and in his next film, *The Breaking Point* (1950), the previously discussed adaptation of *To Have and Have Not*. In his book on Garfield, George Morris describes the scene in which Dan is forced to send Joe away before Bork visits his wrath on them both in retaliation for Dan's unpaid debts. When Dan puts the boy aboard the departing train, Morris writes, his exterior toughness conceals their shared dependence and camaraderie. But as the train disappears in the distance Dan's face is transfigured with the agony of this painful separation from his son, and he "pulls his hat down over his forehead to hide the tears welling up in his eyes."[14] In order to allow the actor to communicate the full impact of this intense moment, director Jean Negulesco wisely kept the camera on Garfield's face in a tight close-up as he walked along the station platform toward the camera.

But apart from the good use he makes of Garfield in this and some other highly charged dramatic scenes, Negulesco's direction of the film is rather undistinguished. As second unit director on the 1932 film of *A Farewell to Arms*, he invested the battle scenes with a high degree of drama and excitement. But his handling of the potentially dramatic and exciting racetrack sequences in the present film, especially the climactic race which ends the picture, is somewhat perfunctory. The location shots at the Auteuil track are clumsily intercut with the studio shots of the actors; as a result these sequences are much less compelling and authentic than they should have been.

Nevertheless, if it is true that the director is responsible for the overall artistic quality of a film, it is also true that a motion picture cannot be significantly better than the screenplay on which it is based; and Casey Robinson's screenplay is simply not in the same class with his script for *The Macomber Affair*. In extending Hemingway's short story for the film, Robinson concentrated too much on multiplying additional plot complications and not enough on inventing incidents calculated to reveal character, to examine motivation more deeply, and to make it easier for the filmgoer to identify with the key characters.

Dan's gradual redemption through the love of Paule and Joe—summed up in his decision to win the race which he had committed himself to lose—could have been delineated in more detail and therefore made to come across more convincingly on the screen. As it is, the combined influence on him of his girl and his son is portrayed in a single exchange between Dan and Paule in which she tells him that "it will kill Joe if you throw that race"; Dan agrees that he owes his son "an honest race." Like Margaret Macomber in *The Macomber Affair*, Dan sees the light a little too quickly to be credible.

But the most serious criticism that can be leveled at *Under My Skin* is the violation of the spirit of Hemingway's story by sparing Joe both his final disillusionment about his father and the loneliness of having no one to turn to for companionship and security at the end. In softening Hemingway's ending, the film misses the point of the story, which is that the lad is going to have to heed his father's warning that "you got to take a lot of things in this life," and be resourceful enough to make it on his own. This is a more touching and true ending to young Joe's story than the one manufactured for the movie.

Under My Skin is a much less accurate rendition of "My Old Man" than *The Macomber Affair* was of "The Short Happy Life of Francis Macomber." It is a wonder, then, that Hemingway dismissed *Macomber* with a condescending anecdote and found *Under My Skin* to be "pretty damn good."[15]

Unless I miss my guess, Hemingway would have liked *My Old Man*, the 1979 TV version of "My Old Man," still better than the 1950 motion picture. Even though TV writer Jerome Kass has performed some major surgery on the Hemingway original, just as Robinson did before him, the resulting film is more satisfying entertainment and thematically closer to Hemingway than the theatrical film of three decades earlier.

This time around Joe Butler becomes Jo Butler so that the role can be enacted by Kristy McNichol, who was cast in the role because she was already known to viewers as the tomboy on a popular TV sitcom. Fair enough, since she comes across in the telefilm as a sturdy young lady cast very much in the same mold as the standard Hemingway apprentice heroes (despite the "sex change"). As such she is quite capable of discerning the good that still lies buried beneath the shabby exterior of her down-at-the-heels father when she is reunited with him at the funeral of her mother, from whom he had been estranged for many years.

As Frank Butler, Jo's dad, Warren Oates turns in another of his flawless performances as a loveable reprobate who responds to his daughter's prodding to resuscitate his moribund career as a racehorse trainer (Oates's build precluded his playing Frank as a jockey). Hemingway's hero, as reincarnated in the TV version of "My Old Man," belongs to a higher order of code hero than his counterpart in either the short story or the earlier movie. The television script suggests that

Frank was the innocent victim of a race track scandal which has unjustly placed him under a cloud with his cronies, and which makes him appear to be more feckless than he really is.

In any event, the film is faithful to Hemingway in indicating that it is Frank's will to vindicate his own youngster's faith in him that motivates him to mend his shattered career and self-respect in order to once more prove himself the thoroughbred human being that he once was. Frank does just that by successfully training an intractable horse named Gilford that every other trainer has despaired of whipping into shape, and training Jo to ride him. In begging Gilford's owner to give the horse another chance, Frank is of course also implicitly asking for an opportunity to prove himself in the bargain; and no one knows this better than he does.

Because of a serious accident at the track, however, Frank is taken to the hospital in critical condition before the big race. As he lies dying, he listens to the race on the radio and lasts long enough to learn that Jo has ridden Gilford to victory.

Except for the pat, not to say contrived, finish of the telemovie, *My Old Man* has all of the qualities of a good Hemingway yarn expertly unraveled. Papa would have been proud of the brittle dialogue, especially the ornery interchanges between father and daughter. When Frank offers the excuse that he gave up trying to see Jo after his divorce because her mother would not allow it, Jo's reply is typically feisty: "You came once—do you call that trying?" At another point, when Jo suggests that Frank occasionally substitute coffee for booze, he answers pointedly: "I don't have any reason to stay awake" and won't until his luck changes.

There are some fine visual metaphors in the telefilm which, along with the screenplay, place it above the general run of conventional made-for-TV movies. When Frank arrives at the home of Jo's aunt after his ex-wife's funeral in order to coax Jo to share his life, her hesitation to comply with his request is registered by her insistence on keeping the screen door between them while they talk. When she finally joins him on the porch, she has equivalently removed the fragile barrier she had temporarily placed between them, and really—if grudgingly—succumbs to his disarming entreaties.

Then they sit together on the front-porch swing, whose swaying suggests the unsteady life to which she is opening herself, just as the tatty mobile home attached to the back end of Frank's truck implies the unsettled existence that may well be hers if her father does not find steady employment. As they start out on their cross-country trek to the track at Saratoga Springs, New York, where Frank hopes to get a permanent job, Jo takes over the wheel to do some of the driving, presaging the fact that she is developing a sense of independence and self-reliance which will serve her well after her father's death—an implication totally in keeping with Hemingway's portrayal of Joe in the story.

In summary, director John Erman's telling visuals are perfectly mated with adapter Kass's pungent dialogue, and that is a very good combination. In addition, Frank Butler emerges in the telefilm as an authentic Hemingway code hero who lives and dies by the code of his profession. A sign at the track reads, "If you're out to have a good time, you can't lose." There is no better way to sum up Hemingway's perennial theme that win or lose, what really counts is how you play the game. In this sense the Frank Butler of the TV version of "My Old Man" is a genuine Hemingway professional, and as such I think Hemingway would have liked him, and the film about him, very much indeed.

All in all, *My Old Man* on television is a better Hemingway adaptation than the 1950 theatrical film based on the same material. The plot and characterization are sharp, the performances consistently of a high order, and the production values superb. The colorful final race, for instance, is staged in an infinitely more exciting fashion than in *Under My Skin*. The cross-cutting between Jo, desperately urging Gilford on to win the race for her father, and Frank, just as desperately trying to hold on to the remaining inches of his life until the race is won, provides an additional dimension of suspense not present in the corresponding sequence in *Under My Skin*, in which Butler's death is completely unexpected.

In expanding Hemingway's short story into a 100-minute, full-length telefilm (excluding commercial breaks) of roughly the same length as the earlier feature film, Kass has remedied the mistake which Casey Robinson made in his adaptation of the same tale by developing the personalities of the key characters in greater depth than was possible in the short story, instead of merely grafting on more plot complications to the story as Robinson did. In consequence, Oates, McNichol, and Eileen Brennan (as Frank's erstwhile girl friend and would-be wife, Marie) are able to create three-dimensional characterizations. Ms. Brennan, it is true, has played coarse, good-natured waitresses like Marie before, notably in *The Last Picture Show* (1971); but no one does it better.

Erman's film, in tandem with Siegel's made-for-TV version of "The Killers," bodes well for future Hemingway adaptations on the tube.

7
Nightmares at Noonday:
The Snows of Kilimanjaro (1952)
and *The Sun Also Rises* (1957)

LIKE "THE SHORT HAPPY LIFE OF FRANCIS
Macomber," "The Snows of Kilimanjaro" was the fruit of
the author's African safari in 1934. Hemingway noted that
he had distilled into it enough material for several stories,
and when Casey Robinson turned "Snows" into a screenplay,
he borrowed material from several of the author's works
—including *A Farewell to Arms* and *The Sun Also Rises*—in
order to expand these compressed episodes and fill out the
film's story line.

"The Snows of Kilimanjaro," like *The Sun Also Rises*, is a
perfect example of the kind of dark tale set in the sunlight
which one critic has dubbed Hemingway's nightmares at
noonday. It records the last hours on earth of a failed writer
named Harry who has contracted a fatal disease in the course
of an African hunting trip. As he lies dying at his jungle
campsite, waiting in vain for a rescue plane to take him to a
hospital, he recalls incidents from his wasted life that are

relayed to the reader in a series of introspective interior monologues.

The story was suggested to Hemingway by the critical bout with dysentery which he suffered on his own safari, and which necessitated a rescue plane being summoned to take him to a hospital for treatment. As the small biplane gained altitude, Hemingway spotted the snowy slopes of Mt. Kilimanjaro. This reminded him of a story which Philip Percival, the expert guide who was leading his safari, had told him about the frozen carcass of a leopard which an explorer had found near one of the peaks of the mountain known as the House of God.

The leopard had apparently gone astray while pursuing a mountain goat. In writing his short story, Hemingway employed Percival's anecdote as a parable with which he prefaced his tale; however, he noted that whatever prize had driven that intrepid animal to climb so high would forever remain a mystery. The detail about the mountain goat was suppressed because thematically Hemingway wanted to use the leopard's prowess in climbing ever upward and onward to reach an unspecified goal as a sharp contrast to Harry's earthbound and futile strivings to fulfill his lofty aspirations to scale artistic heights and become a great writer.

One usually gets the kind of death one deserves. The leopard perished nobly in the pure, rarefied atmosphere of Kilimanjaro's snows striving for something above and beyond it. Harry dies ignobly on the hot, dusty plain far below Kilimanjaro's summit because his reach had never exceeded his grasp.

Harry blames his rich wife for destroying his artistic talent, but in his heart of hearts he knows that he himself had carelessly allowed wealth and luxury to eat away at his writing ability, just as gangrene is now eating away at his infected leg. The African safari was Harry's last-ditch effort to regain his artistic integrity by trying to "work the fat off his soul" the way a fighter goes into training in order to burn the fat off his body.¹ But by that time it was already too late for Harry to accomplish this, and his physical death simply reinforces the finality of his artistic demise.

Hemingway had similarly feared that the standard of living to which he had become accustomed since marrying his wealthy second wife, Pauline, might make him lazy and unproductive; and his private reason for writing "Snows" was to provide a continuing warning for himself never to allow his creative talent to atrophy in the way that Harry did. He firmly believed that the hardest thing for any writer to do was to survive long enough "to get his work done."² Harry did not do so.

Harry is an apprentice hero who suffers from a case of arrested development, for he remains adolescent and self-centered throughout his life. In the short story Hemingway provided no code hero to serve as an inspiration for Harry, but Casey Robinson created for the film version a character who is tantamount to Hemingway's concept of a code hero. As Henry King, the director of the picture, told me: "We needed a guidepost for Harry to follow in the film, someone to remind Harry of how he was falling short of his aspirations. Hemingway has such a figure in many of his stories, and Harry's Uncle Bill was created to be such a guidepost in the film of *Snows*."

At this point in time Darryl Zanuck, who had been a fixture at Fox in one administrative capacity or another since the thirties, had his own unit at the studio and was independently making pictures for Fox release. Zanuck had acquired the short story from Hemingway for $75,000 and assigned Robinson to be the producer of the picture and to write the screenplay (though Robinson received screen credit only for the latter function), while he himself served as overall executive producer of the film.

Robinson decided to fill out Hemingway's highly compressed short story by direct presentation of Harry's recollections about his past life as formally dramatized flashbacks in the film. But, as Edward Murray astutely notes in *The Cinematic Imagination* (1972), Harry's recollections of his past life in the short story are *not* flashbacks at all; they are interior monologues in which Hemingway portrays Harry reflecting and commenting on his past experiences as he lies dying. Robinson sought to retain the subjective dimension of these memories—not an easy thing to do in a film, as Graham Greene has noted—by having Harry comment, voice-over, on the events portrayed in the flashbacks.

Robinson, moreover, expanded the flashback material in the film by including not only those events to which Harry refers in his reveries about his past in the story but also by borrowing additional material from Hemingway's other fiction. "When I read the script," said Henry King, "I couldn't tell where Hemingway left off and Casey Robinson began." King recalls that after Hemingway saw the film he said, "I sold Fox a single story, not my complete works. This movie has something from nearly every story that I ever wrote in it."

Though the comment is an example of typically Hemingway-esque exaggeration, it contained more than a kernel of truth. However, Robinson's approach to writing the screenplay was legitimate. As noted in the discussion of Hotchner's script for *Hemingway's Adventures of a Young Man*, the apprentice heroes of Hemingway's key works are blood relatives of each other who share in common Nick Adam's childhood, adolescence, and young manhood as the background of their own individual lives. In fact, the first flashback episode of *Snows* is partially derived from the Nick Adams story entitled "The End of Something," in which Nick takes his girl on a fishing trip with a view to breaking off their relationship before they return home that evening.

King liked the concept of the episode, but thought it too lengthy as Robinson had written it in the screenplay. "The way Casey had written the sequence," King remarked, "it took thirty pages when it should have taken ten. Harry and the girl caught and cooked a fish; and then he went home and quarrelled with his uncle over the girl and finally decided to give her up at his uncle's urging. I told Casey that this long sequence was deadly and would put the audience to sleep." King proposed that at the point where Harry (Gregory Peck)

Johnson (Torin Thatcher), Cynthia (Ava Gardner), and Harry (Gregory Peck) stalk big game in *The Snows of Kilimanjaro* (1952), directed by Henry King. To extend Hemingway's short story into a feature-length film the script drew on several other Hemingway works, to the extent that after seeing the film Hemingway quipped, "I sold Fox a single story, not my complete works." The scene pictured here was suggested by material from "The Short Happy Life of Francis Macomber." (The Museum of Modern Art/Film Stills Archive)

introduces the flashback by telling his wife, Helen (Susan Hayward), that there are plenty of things in his past which he has never told her, there should be a quick cut to a long shot of Harry as a young man standing in the shadows on the front porch of the house in which he lives with his uncle (Leo G. Carroll). He is calling to his girl as she runs away.

Then the boy goes back into the living room and stands silhouetted in the doorway as his Uncle Bill convinces him to let the girl go. "We'll do the scene with a seventeen-year-old boy standing in for Greg Peck," King concluded; "but we'll dub in Greg's voice speaking in a somewhat higher, younger register; and we'll have Greg Peck at seventeen." Robinson came back in an hour with the sequence cut down to seven pages, King said, "and it was just what I wanted. Though he hadn't used any of the preliminary snatches of dialogue that I had sketched out for him, he had conceptualized what I had said and put it on paper in his own words."

In the scene as finally written, Uncle Bill uses a very Hemingway-esque metaphor to sum up his plea that Harry not ruin his young life and potential career by getting involved with the tawdry girl who had just left the house. Becoming a genuine writer, says Uncle Bill, "is a lifelong and lonely safari; and the prey which the writer seeks is a truth worth telling." Uncle Bill ends with this plea: "I beg you not to ruin yourself before you start by loading your pack with excess baggage."

But Harry unfortunately does just that. He lives an aimless life in Europe and squanders his serious creative talent—until he meets Cynthia (Ava Gardner), a woman of real substance whose willingness to share his poverty in a Paris tenement encourages him to renew his struggles to master his craft. This interlude, in which Harry and Cynthia live on Paris's Left Bank after World War I and attend the bullfights in Spain, owes some of its material to similar scenes in *The Sun Also Rises*. What's more, the character of Cynthia has much in common with Lady Brett Ashley of *Sun*. But

Cynthia is also drawn from one of Harry's reveries in "The Snows of Kilimanjaro," in which he recalls a girl whom he had loved and foolishly lost, and who still painfully perdures in his memory as the one true love of his life.

In the short story, we are not told precisely how Harry came to lose this girl, so Robinson was free to improvise on this point by combining elements from other Hemingway fictional works. According to the screenplay, Cynthia accompanies Harry on an African hunting expedition reminiscent of the one in "The Short Happy Life of Francis Macomber." During the safari she becomes increasingly convinced that Harry will never be content to settle down to the kind of domestic life which she craves, and that she will not be able to keep up with his incessant globe-trotting in search of material for his books. She therefore fears that she will inevitably become for Harry the sort of "excess baggage" that will tie him down and hamper his development as a creative writer.

By the time they arrive in Spain for the bullfights, Cynthia has determined to leave Harry; and she walks out on him at the conclusion of the touching nightclub scene in which she attempts to make Harry believe that she is jilting him for a slick Spanish flamenco dancer.

In a curious variation on both *A Farewell to Arms* and *For Whom the Bell Tolls*, Cynthia volunteers to drive an ambulance for the Loyalists during the Spanish civil war and Harry joins one of the Loyalist brigades as a soldier. Like Frederic Henry, Cynthia is an ambulance driver; and like Robert Jordan, Cynthia and Harry are working for the Loyalist cause. In a somewhat too pat coincidence Harry accidentally encounters Cynthia dying of a shell wound on the battlefield. The medics carry her away on a stretcher, and she disappears like a fading apparition into a cloud of gunsmoke, leaving Harry behind once and for all.

The film at this point returns to the plot of "The Snows of Kilimanjaro" by drawing on Harry's recollections of how he desperately followed women on the street who resembled his lost beloved, only to be disappointed each time; in this way Harry meets his wealthy wife, Helen, for the first time. It is with Helen that Harry makes his second safari, in the hope that in the disciplined regimen of the hunt he can hunt down and recapture the essence of his talent.

The inspiration to make the trip to Africa comes from Uncle Bill who, shortly before his death, gives Harry a slip of paper on which he has written the legend of the leopard that perished in the snows of Mt. Kilimanjaro. "Perhaps the leopard took the wrong trail and followed the wrong scent and got lost and died," a friendly bartender (Marcel Dalio) suggests as the explanation of the riddle. Harry agrees that this is the meaning that Uncle Bill meant for him to take from the parable; he returns to Africa to get back on the right track, realizing that since Cynthia's death he has in fact become the hack writer his uncle had warned him against becoming.

Up to this point in the film, the way in which the screenplay has extended Hemingway's original short story has been in keeping with its spirit. But the last portion of the movie departs seriously from Hemingway's intent by leaving the distinct impression that Harry will live to profit from the insights he has gleaned from the examination of his wasted life. Throughout the short story Hemingway utilizes the presence of buzzards hovering in a tree near Harry's tent and of a marauding hyena—creatures known to feed on carrion—in order to signal Harry's impending demise; and Hemingway ends the story with Helen discovering Harry's lifeless body, as a hyena howls in the night.

The movie deliberately negates the story's clear foreshadowing of Harry's death by the symbolic buzzards and hyena: Helen drives the prowling hyena away from the tent during the night, and Harry awakens in the morning to see that the birds have flown away from the tree, just as the rescue plane is landing to take him to a hopsital. The import of the ending of the film, then, is that Harry will live to pick up the pieces of both his shattered writing career and his splintered marriage.

Henry King completely endorsed the upbeat ending of the film because he felt that though it is not in keeping with the way in which Hemingway ended his story it had at least been sufficiently prepared for during the concluding scenes of the movie; they establish that Helen will now serve as the kind of sympathetic emotional support for Harry that Cynthia had always been, and that with Helen's help Harry will make good his resolution to start life afresh.

"When Helen met Harry," King explained, "she was a spoiled rich woman. But by the time of the safari she is truly in love with Harry; and that makes her put up a valiant fight for his life, tending his wounded leg and nursing him through his spasms of delirium. Only a woman who was desperately in love could do that. And so the picture ends with this little ray of hope that she will at last completely replace Cynthia in his life, the woman whom he lost."

At the time of the film's release in 1952, Casey Robinson, who had once more supplied an upbeat ending for a Hemingway movie, went much farther than King in defending the movie's positive ending by maintaining that it is completely compatible with the theme of Hemingway's story. According to Robinson, Hemingway's intent was to say that "any of us have earned a fitting reward if we have the honesty to add up our mistakes, and have a deeply felt wish to correct them." In the film, Robinson contended, that reward takes the form of Harry's getting a second chance to reform his life and save his marriage.[3]

But the point of the story, as most of its interpreters see it, is that Harry's tragedy is precisely that of a person coming to grips with the failures of his life, with the help of the keener insight that one acquires on the brink of death, just when, ironically enough, it is too late to profit in any practical way by this new-found self-knowledge. Hemingway's point, as Anthony Burgess has rightly expressed it, is that, before Harry dies, he "faces his failure to serve both art and life without self-pity, with understanding, submission to destiny," having in death at last come to terms with his misspent life and "burned the fat off his soul."[4] For Hemingway, Harry's reward at the end of the story is his spiritual salvation; for Robinson, however, Harry's reward in the film is a much more material one, since it involves being reconciled with his rich wife.

Since Hemingway's powerful ending did not survive in the film, he wryly commented when the film opened that he planned to oil up his hunting rifle, return to Africa, and climb Mt. Kilimanjaro in search of the soul of Darryl Zanuck; he admitted, however, that he had not seen the film in its entirety.[5] Although some critics thought that Harry's survival in the film was made real and moving, the film's ending is ultimately no match for the Hemingway original. Nonetheless this undeniable fact should not be allowed to overshadow the equally incontestable fact that like *The Macomber Affair*, the movie for most of its running time "goes the distance"—to use a favorite Hemingway expression—as a respectable rendition of the author's fiction; employing judiciously chosen segments of his dialogue throughout, it is a carefully crafted movie.

With the exception of some second unit work filmed in advance in the African veldt by a Hollywood crew, the picture was actually shot in forty-eight days almost entirely on the Fox sound stages in Hollywood. Cinematographer Leon Shamroy, for whom *Snows* was the ninth of fourteen films photographed for King, has said that he was very proud of the authentic look of the movie: "Almost every foot of it was shot in the studio, even those night shots under the mountain, some of the best ever done; and nobody guessed for a moment it wasn't all taking place in Africa."[6]

King worked out some stunnning visual metaphors in the film, the most impressive of which is the way that the stages of the relationship of Harry and Cynthia are marked by fire imagery. On the night that Harry and Cynthia meet, he lights her cigarette as they stand in a dark Paris street; and the flare of the match symbolizes the flame of love that has been kindled between them. Later, when Cynthia has decided to break up with Harry in the Spanish nightclub, the candle on their table stands in the foreground of the shot, its unsteady flame foreshadowing the guttering out of their relationship. Finally, when Harry finds Cynthia dying on the battlefield, the smoke and flame ignited by the shells bursting around them signals that their relationship is now being permanently destroyed.

The film was carefully cast, even in the most minor roles. Marcel Dalio, who played the owner of the café in Hawks's *To Have and Have Not* (1944), appears here as the bartender of the Paris bistro who explains to Harry the meaning of Uncle Bill's parable about the leopard. He would again play a bartender for King in *The Sun Also Rises* (1957), but King said that Dalio's appearance in similar roles in three different Hemingway films was a coincidence, and that he was not trying to establish any covert continuity among the Hemingway films by casting Dalio in his two Hemingway motion pictures: "He seemed to me to be the fellow for the part in each case, particularly because he was a native Frenchman; and he just happened to be a contract player at Fox at the time that I made *Snows* and *Sun*."

Although Gregory Peck's part in *Snows* was to mark a peak in the actor's career, King remembered that Peck at first declined the role. After reading the script, Peck told King, with whom he had already made several pictures, that he wanted to work with him again, but not on *The Snows of Kilimanjaro*. "He had been in *The Macomber Affair* and that had been a box office disaster," King recalled. "And so he vowed never again to appear in another Hemingway picture, especially one told in flashback and adapted by Casey Robinson, who had done *Macomber*. I assured him that I was pleased with the screenplay and that I would like it even better when we had polished it some more. So Greg agreed to make the movie on my recommendation, because he said that he was afraid I would do a good picture without him and he would be sorry that he had passed up the chance to be in it. And of course he gave a grand performance.

"*The Snows of Kilimanjaro* wrote a new ticket for Ava Gardner," King continued, by catapulting her into international stardom. "At first Zanuck didn't want to use her because he said a lot of people in Hollywood thought that she was a beautiful girl but a lousy actress. But she had just gotten good notices for playing the old Helen Morgan part in *Show Boat*, and so he phoned her. She said that she wanted very badly to do the part and to do it well."

Ava Gardner later explained that she had grown tired of playing what she deemed to be a string of "bitches and tramps," a cycle which had been inaugurated by her performance in *The Killers* in 1946; and when she was offered the role of Cynthia she was consequently anxious to play "a good average girl with normal impulses." Moreover, as Judith Kass comments in her book on Ava Gardner: "Given her own insecurities, her ego needed the reinforcement that a veteran director could give her. Henry King was just such a veteran."[7]

Asked to comment on this statement, King responded, "I always enjoyed working with Ava. She was no playgirl who didn't want to work; she took her roles seriously. While working with her on *Snows* I learned her acting style. She is no tragedian, but when she is playing a character that she understands she has the ability, when doing a serious emotional scene, to project that she is bleeding inside without shedding a single tear. Some actresses ham it up and drown a sad scene in tears, but Ava doesn't have to cry on the screen to make the moviegoer cry. She proves that old maxim that when all the tears are on the actor's face there aren't any on the audience's faces.

"When we came to the scene in the Spanish night club, in which Cynthia walks out of Harry's life because she thinks that she is an obstacle to his success as a serious writer, we rehearsed and rehearsed it with Greg and Ava sitting at the table. After they both felt completely relaxed, I filmed the whole scene in a single take without close-ups. I was so moved by Ava's performance that I didn't even want to do a second take. But we did another one just to be safe; and when I ran them both with my editor, Barbara McLean, she was so overwhelmed by the first take that she said she didn't even remember seeing the second one. Ava made me feel that I had photographed her soul in that scene, and for me it was the top sequence of the picture."

Barbara McLean had, like Leon Shamroy, worked with King often in the past; but when he advised her that he wanted to have the flashbacks edited in what was at that time considered to be an innovative way, she balked. "I told her that I wanted no dissolves to tip off the audience that a flashback was beginning or ending, just a straight cut from

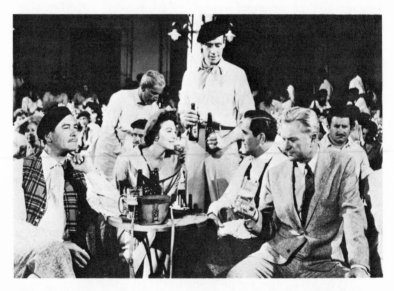

Mike Campbell (Errol Flynn), Brett Ashley (Ava Gardner), Robert Cohn (Mel Ferrer), Jake Barnes (Tyrone Power), and Bill Gorton (Eddie Albert) attend a fiesta in Pamplona in Henry King's *The Sun Also Rises* (1957). A stickler for realism, Hemingway worried that audiences would notice that the film was shot in Mexico instead of in Spain where the story was set. (The Museum of Modern Art/Film Stills Archive)

one scene to the next. She said that Mr. Zanuck wouldn't like that; and I replied that that was the way that the short story had been told, with abrupt cuts back and forth in time, and that I wanted to follow that pattern in the movie. When Zanuck ran the rough cut, he assumed that the cutter hadn't had a chance to put in the dissolves yet, but planned to do so later. He told her not to because the film was marvelous without them. He thought that doing away with the dissolves for the flashbacks was his idea; and I never told him otherwise."

Critic Lionel Godfrey writes that *The Snows of Kilimanjaro* is in many ways "a remarkable achievement, with its restrained but expressive use of hunting as symbolism and its cutting from time-present to time-past."[8] Despite Hemingway's jibes about the film, which he liked to refer to as *The Snows of Zanuck*, the picture was marked by the contributions of several talented artists. Besides Robinson's fundamentally literate script and Shamroy's exquisite color photography, the film also boasted an extraordinary score by Bernard Herrmann, which ranges from Spanish and African rhythms to the cool jazz which defines the sensuous atmosphere of the Parisian café scene in which Harry and Cynthia fall in love.

Although in the original story Harry refers to Cynthia in his remembrances of things past, she is not portrayed directly in his reveries. As noted previously, Robinson therefore developed her character along the lines of Lady Brett Ashley in *The Sun Also Rises*, another lost twenties girl. Robinson says that he saw Cynthia as "a kind of doomed character" who like Lady Brett had the capacity to stick out her chin and absorb whatever shocks she was given by life, "and to do it with a kind of pathetic laugh."[9] Given the affinity between Cynthia and Lady Brett Ashley, it is not surprising that Ava Gardner turned up playing Lady Brett in King's film adaptation of *The Sun Also Rises* five years later, when she would again garner accolades for a superior performance.

King met Hemingway for the first time in Paris in the

mid-twenties, at the time that Hemingway was working on the novel that was to become *The Sun Also Rises*. "It was in a honky tonk in Rue Fontaine which I discovered while I was researching a picture in Europe," King recalled; "it was a tavern where Hemingway frequently used to go. The girl that was the source of Lady Brett in the novel was there with him at his table that night."

The young woman in question was Lady Duff Twysden, a self-indulgent, promiscuous thirty-two-year-old Englishwoman who together with several other of Hemingway's friends and acquaintances in those days provided the real-life patterns for the principal characters in *The Sun Also Rises*. Cayetano Ordóñez, known popularly as Niño de la Palma, was the model for the bullfighter Pedro Romero, whom the novelist named for a great eighteenth-century matador. Hemingway himself was in many ways associated with the hero of the novel, Jake Barnes. Like Hemingway, Jake was wounded in Italy during World War I and lived for some time in Europe after the war. Jake, however, was rendered impotent by his war wound; but even this was indirectly a spin-off from Hemingway's own experience.

In addition to suffering a leg wound at Fossalta, Hemingway discovered that bits of cloth from his uniform had infected his scrotum; he therefore had to spend a portion of his recuperation period in the hospital's genitourinary ward. There he met a lad who had lost his penis but retained his testicles, meaning that, as the author put it, "he was capable of all normal feelings as a *man*, but incapable of consummating them."[10] This is precisely the frustration Jake Barnes feels in his hopeless love for the nymphomaniacal Brett, who futilely seeks in promiscuity to assuage the desolation occasioned by the death of her true love in the war.

The plot of *The Sun Also Rises* had its source in the fiesta of San Fermín in Pamplona, which Hemingway and his party of friends attended in the summer of 1925. A scant two weeks after the festival ended, Hemingway set about immortalizing the experiences of the trip in his first major novel. Though some of the happenings in the novel were only thinly disguised versions of real events, the novelist's imagination substantially altered many others for the purposes of art. For example, Hemingway's wife Hadley, who does not appear in the novel in any way, developed a harmless crush on the matador Ordóñez; and in the novel Hemingway transmuted this minor incident into Brett's brief affair with Romero, giving rise to Duff Twysden's subsequent complaint that, unlike Brett, she had never slept with "the bloody bullfighter."[11]

Pedro Romero is manifestly the code hero of the novel, for Romero is quintessentially a man of honor, both in and out of the ring. "In Spain honor is a very real thing," Hemingway explains in his 1932 book on bullfighting, *Death in the Afternoon*. "Called *pundonor*, it means honor, probity, courage, self-respect, and pride in one word."[12] The moral dimension of Romero's code of honor is exemplified when ex-boxer Robert Cohn bests the matador in a fistfight over Brett. Romero scores a moral victory not only in standing up with dignity to an opponent who is his superior in size and physical strength but in later sincerely offering to make an honest woman of Brett in marriage. Romero's chivalry in turn prompts Brett to renounce him long before her infatuation for him has run its course, so that she will not be "one of these bitches who ruins children."[13]

Moreover, Jake, the apprentice hero of the novel, clearly respects Romero's integrity and is ashamed that he is not more like him. In the course of the novel Jake shows his growing spiritual kinship with Romero by becoming increasingly more adept at disciplining his emotions as Romero does; and in this way Jake learns to live with both his wound and his world. That Romero is still in his late teens and Jake in his late twenties shows once more that in Hemingway's view the difference between an apprentice hero and a code hero is not one of age.

In their irresponsible carousing and decadent behavior throughout much of the book, Jake and his companions demonstrate a lack of the maturity evident in the younger Romero. They are all members of the postwar group of expatriates, America's "lost generation"; Jake's impotency is a metaphor for the spiritual condition of these emotionally exhausted, physically sterile individuals who, like himself, are awash in postwar disillusionment and unable to sustain any fruitful and lasting relationships.

Hemingway reports in his autobiographical account of his postwar Paris days, *A Moveable Feast*, published posthumously in 1964, that the phrase *lost generation*, which he had toyed with as a possible title for the novel, was quoted to him by Getrude Stein. She said that the owner of an auto repair shop had coined it in speaking of an inept young mechanic, to indicate that the young people who lost the best years of their lives in the war would never get them back. "All of you young people who served in the war," she inveighed; "you are all a lost generation."[14]

Although Hemingway employed Gertrude Stein's remark as an epigraph for the novel, the title of the work was finally derived from the book's second epigraph, from Ecclesiastes, which Hemingway meant to offset the pessimism of the first epigraph. This Old Testament quotation states that although the sun rises and sets and generations come and go, the earth abides forever, indicating how life goes on despite individual human misfortune and failure. For as Hemingway confessed to his editor, Maxwell Perkins, he had "a great deal of fondness and admiration for the earth, and not a hell of a lot for my generation."[15]

Hemingway asked F. Scott Fitzgerald for his comments on the manuscript, and at the latter's urging he lopped off the first 3,700 words of the novel, which gave superfluous background material on the chief characters. Although Hemingway agreed with Fitzgerald's criticism of *Sun*, he resented his fellow writer for being right and later denied that

Fitzgerald had in any way helped him to improve the novel. As if to "even the score" between them, Hemingway made a condescending reference about Fitzgerald being naively enamoured of the rich in "The Snows of Kilimanjaro" when it first appeared in a magazine in 1936. Fitzgerald was deeply offended and asked that his name be deleted from the story when it was reprinted, and Hemingway grudgingly complied. Clearly it was perilous to help Hemingway with his work in any way, as others too found out to their cost, and Fitzgerald made the mistake of making valuable suggestions about several of Hemingway's works.

The novel was both a critical and a popular success, yet it was not acquired for filming until several years after it was published. "I bought it fifteen years before I sold it to Zanuck," Howard Hawks has said. "I thought it was hard to do. It was about a fellow who was impotent."[16] When in the forties he purchased the screen rights for $10,000 from Hemingway's first wife, Hadley, to whom the novelist had turned over the rights as part of their divorce settlement, Hawks decided that movie censors would not approve a script that dealt with this delicate topic. By the time Zanuck bought the rights from Hawks for $200,000, however, movies had become mature enough for the censors to countenance such a theme.

"At this point Zanuck was still an independent producer releasing pictures through Fox," Henry King recalled. "He wanted me to do *The Sun Also Rises* and sent me Peter Viertel's script. I responded that I had always liked the book and that, although it was a long time since I had read it, I was sure that this script was not Hemingway. Zanuck had also sent a script to Ava Gardner who lived in Spain near the place where Hemingway was staying at the time. She showed the screenplay to Hemingway, saying, 'For your own pride you have to read it and change things. Everyone in the script runs around saying, "*C'est la guerre*," and peachy things like that.' "[17] After summoning Viertel to Mardrid for a confer-

ence about the script, Hemingway decided that the script
needed major overhauling which no amount of minor revisions could accomplish.

"Hemingway wired Zanuck that if the script was shot as
it was he would sue, because it wasn't his story," said King.
"So the studio got another writer; but he knew nothing about
bullfighting, and got the technical details about it all wrong. I
refused to direct the revised script because it now had nothing
at all to do with Hemingway and was all wrong about
bullfighting as well. I told Zanuck that I was not a student of
Hemingway, but that I knew this book; and it seemed to me
that neither of the writers who had worked on the script so far
had read the book carefully. So I said that I was going to see
that the next person who worked on the script was going to
get *inside* the novel.

"The next morning I started with page one of the book
and page one of the script, and blocked out the script with
cross-references to the novel. I went back and forth between
the two, deleting scenes from the script that weren't based on
Hemingway and replacing them with references to scenes in
the novel that should be dramatized instead."

King then met with Peter Viertel and Zanuck in London,
and they locked themselves in a hotel room at Claridge's for
four days while Viertel wrote the scenes that King had
indicated should be brought over from the book into the
screenplay. When the trio emerged from their self-imposed
seclusion, they learned that Hemingway would soon be
sailing from France aboard the *Ile de France* and that his boat
was scheduled to dock overnight at Liverpool before crossing
the Atlantic.

"Peter and I drove down to Liverpool and met his ship,"
King continued, "and handed him the finished script on
board. After we had dinner in his stateroom, we sat up half
the night while he read every word of the screenplay."
Hemingway ultimately expressed pleasure that the new script
was a notable improvement over the earlier version he had

perused in Spain, and he agreed that it was much closer to the book. "We were delighted, and drove back to London feeling that our mission had been accomplished."

The final shooting script does contain most of the crucial scenes in the novel and carefully selected passages of its dialogue. But that does not mean that King's screen version of *The Sun Also Rises* is without difficulties. As has been previously pointed out, much of the power of Hemingway's writing resides in what he leaves unsaid; that is, in his ability to imply much more meaning than he explicitly spells out on the printed page.

The sense of a scene in a Hemingway story is "embedded neither in the speeches nor in the action," Arthur Knight explains, but in the cluster of connotations arising from "the overtones of words on paper, as Hemingway had learned to use them."[18] Therefore, although some of the deeper implications of the novel are apparent in the film, others are not.

On the one hand, the impotency of Jake (Tyrone Power) comes across in the film, as it does in the novel, as symbolizing the incapacity of the disillusioned postwar generation to feel and to love deeply; Jake's abiding respect for Romero (Robert Evans) also comes through in the film, as does his consequent recognition of the bullfighter as the norm of conduct against which he judges himself and his companions, Mike Campbell (Errol Flynn), Robert Cohn (Mel Ferrer), and Bill Gorton (Eddie Albert).

On the other hand, at least one dimension of Hemingway's vision as expressed in the novel does not surface in the movie. Hemingway's ethical code, it has been noted, amounts to a kind of natural religion rooted in the pantheistic concept that the most intimate contact one can have with God on this earth is to be found wherever nature has remained as yet uncontaminated by the encroachments of modern mechanized society. Such communion with nature purifies Hemingway's heroes.

In the novel Jake and Bill Gorton share this spiritually

refreshing experience on a fishing expedition in the untrammeled Spanish countryside before going on to the fiesta in Pamplona. Hemingway deliberately depicts this tranquil sojourn as a clear contrast to the decadent, frantic revelry of the Paris and Pamplona scenes. Unfortunately, the deeper meaning which this return to nature has for the pair, the meaning Hemingway implanted "in the white spaces between the lines," does not come through in the movie at all.

Instead, their interlude comes across as a routine fishing trip out of *Field and Stream*. It is just such unspoken thematic resonances that Ben Hecht had in mind when he said that the trouble with adapting Hemingway to the screen was that "the son-of-a-bitch writes on water." Nailing down the deeper nuances of the fishing sequence simply eluded the cooks who boiled up the screenplay of *The Sun Also Rises*.

Jake and Bill still cling to some kind of natural religion in the book; but the debauched Brett is pictured as having lost all sense of spiritual values, and she is manifestly uneasy when Jake takes her to visit a cathedral in order to wistfully recall his own abandoned religious faith. Yet the movie script gives her religious convictions which she does not possess in the book. "Hemingway's Brett is depicted as a pagan goddess reigning over a wasteland," Edward Murray comments, but the movie Brett "prays devoutly at the altar for Romero."[19]

As a result, one of Brett's key remarks at the end of the movie—it is taken directly from the book—seems to be at odds with the religious faith she seems to display in the cathedral scene. She tells Jake that the sense of well-being she has experienced attendant on her renunciation of Romero is "what we have instead of God." But as she is presented in the film she seems to have God, too.

The significance of one of her other interchanges with Jake in the film's last scene also seems to be inconsistent with what has gone before. Over and over again in the film, as in the book, the pair articulate their mutual despair of ever forging a satisfying relationship. Brett assumes that the only problem is Jake's impotence, but Jake sees the situation differently. He becomes gradually aware that both he and Brett came out of the war unable to love genuinely ever again; and he knows that there is no "cure" for what ails them because they have both lost the moral and emotional stamina required to sustain a deep, lasting relationship—and that this would be true even if he were not physically impotent. The novel ends with Jake stoically accepting this fact.

Yet in the last lines of the movie Jake assures Brett that she is right in believing that "there must be some answer for us somewhere." Obviously there is none; and perhaps the moviemakers assumed that perceptive filmgoers would infer that Jake is only deceiving himself by agreeing with Brett —who is no more capable of change than he is—that there is still a chance for them. Even if such is the case, the ending of the film still runs counter to Hemingway's intent, however; by the end of the novel Jake has learned to stop deceiving himself and to shed all of his romantic illusions about life, including those involving himself and Brett. Hence, no matter how one looks at it, the ending of the movie is contrary to the inner logic of the story as Hemingway designed it.

Film critics scolded King and company for botching the ending of the movie when it was released in 1957, as well as for cribbing material from *A Farewell to Arms* in the wartime flashbacks in the film. But on this latter point the moviemakers must in fairness be defended for the same reasons that applied to the use of *Farewell* in the screenplay of *The Snows of Kilimanjaro*, and most particularly in the script of *Hemingway's Adventures of a Young Man*.

First of all, there are the usual parallels between Jake and Barnes and Frederic Henry as typical Hemingway apprentice heroes who are in effect older versions of Nick Adams (Frederic's experiences in the Italian army and Jake's experiences as an expatriate in postwar Europe clearly build, in each case, on Nick's). Secondly, there are similar parallels between Brett Ashley and Catherine Barkley. Brett and Catherine are both British in background; each loved and lost a soldier in the war; each was a nurse in an Italian hospital, where she fell in love with the hero of the novel while he was recuperating from a battle injury. Given the continuity between the principal characters of these two novels, then, there seems to be ample justification for the screenplay of *The Sun Also Rises* to draw on *A Farewell to Arms* to fill in the details of the flashbacks which portray how Jake and Brett met and fell in love while she was nursing him in the hospital—before he learned of his impotence and broke off their relationship.

Although Jake's reveries about how he met and lost Brett take the form of subjective interior monologues in the novel, King presents the hero's recollections in the film as flashbacks which directly dramatize the events that he is thinking about in the novel—which is, of course, the same approach that King took in treating Harry's memories in the film of *Snows*. The flashbacks in *Sun* are presumably seen from the hero's point of view, as were the flashbacks in *Snows*, beginning and ending as they do with Jake lying on his bed recalling these painful memories. To that extent Jake seems to be the narrator of the film; yet neither of the voices who speak over the sound track in the opening moments of the movie can be identified as that of Tyrone Power in the role of Jake.

The first narrator has the voice of an older man which is clearly meant to approximate Hemingway's own, as was that of the narrator of *Hemingway's Adventures*. This first narrator, accompanied by shots of a sunrise, solemnly intones the excerpt from Ecclesiastes used as one of the two epigraphs of the novel; and he returns at the end of the picture to repeat these lines. A second, younger voice follows that of the first narrator at the beginning of the movie and delivers some remarks, over shots of some Parisian streets, that refer to the other epigraph of the novel drawn from Gertrude Stein: "Our story deals with the Paris of 1922, shortly after what used to be called the Great War. We were part of that lost generation who continued to live as if they were about to die." Then he adds, "It was here thirty-five years ago that I first met Jake Barnes."

In the scene that follows Jake meets on the street a disabled veteran named Harris, and their conversation about their experiences in the war foreshadows the later revelation of Jake's impotence. Harris then disappears from the film for good.

When I asked Henry King what the audience is to make of the two narrators who open the film, and whether Harris was supposed to represent the young Hemingway on his way home from the war, he replied: "One can presume that the first voice is that of the author of the novel, the one who conceived the telling of that phase of our lives which followed the Great War. World War I caused many changes in the world as we had known it up to that time, and this man depicted that era for us in his work. Next comes the voice of the particular individual who is actually telling the story we are about to see unfold on the screen. He is not any one definite character in the film; rather he is presented as someone who knew all of the characters and who is now going to tell us what happened to them. The veteran whom Jake meets in the first scene is not supposed to represent the young Hemingway or anybody else; he is there simply to acquaint the audience with Jake's war experiences."

A more effective approach to the opening narration would have been to let Jake serve as the narrator, rather than some undefined, disembodied individual. Jake's acting as narrator at the beginning of the film would have provided continuity with the flashbacks which occur later in the movie, and would also have supplied a better hook on which to hang the movie's single fantasy sequence. In that sequence, as Murray has pointed out, Jake's jealousy of Romero's masculinity is projected in a quick succession of subjective shots of bullfight posters in which Romero's image seems to grow progressively larger as Jake looks up at each of them. (The implicit association of Romero with a virile bull and of Jake with an impotent steer, is made elsewhere in the movie.) The sequence ends with Jake drunkenly hurling a glass of blood-red wine at the matador's image. Ashamed of this pathetic display of self-pity, he sinks back in his chair at a sidewalk café.

In sum, establishing Jake from the outset of the film as the character from whose frame of reference the entire story is being told would have enabled the audience more easily to identify with him and his problems throughout the film and would have served to approximate to some degree at least the way in which the novel makes use of a first-person narration by Jake. Film historian Roy Pickard's comment that the script of *The Sun Also Rises* is not as well constructed as that of *The Snows of Kilimanjaro* seems accurate. "What really sinks the film is the casting," he goes on, because actors like Tyrone Power, Errol Flynn, and Mel Ferrer were "too old for their parts."[20]

"The story takes place several years *after* the war," King said in reply to this opinion. "Besides, they were supposed to look dissipated and worn out, and this dimension of their personalities would have been lost if we had used younger actors." Many critics singled out Errol Flynn's performance in particular as the high-water mark of his acting career. Although at least one reviewer sneered that Flynn was simply playing himself, Philip Roth, who liked little else about the movie, expressed admiration in his article on the film in *The New Republic* for Flynn's compelling performance as the dissolute but somehow likeable Mike Campbell.

The director had heard that Flynn was a hard drinker and a womanizer; "but that was all on the surface," said King. "Underneath he was a serious, hard-working actor. He showed in his soliloquy about temporarily losing Brett to Romero near the end of the picture the way a man really feels when his girl has left him. That scene was in the back of his mind from the first day of shooting. Acting did not come easily to him; he usually tended to rush through a long and difficult scene just to get the agony over with. But we would talk for hours about Mike's state of mind in that scene. I told him not to worry about projecting the emotions of the scene because once he had thought his interpretation through the emotions would take care of themselves; and that is what happened. We did his long speech all on the first take, like Ava's long nightclub scene in *Snows*. Flynn was nominated for an Oscar for his performance in *Sun*, and he deserved to have won it."

Flynn, Lionel Godfrey has written, "was much more than the ham he and others pretended he was"; and his portrayal of Mike Campbell "was memorable, as though the character had stepped out of Hemingway's novel."[21] Yet Hemingway's only specific comment on the film was to smirk, "Any picture in which Errol Flynn is the best actor is its own worst enemy."[22] Once again it should be mentioned that Hemingway's opinion of a movie was based on having seen only a part of it. He walked out on *Sun* after half an hour, which means that he did not get a chance to see much of Flynn's performance, or of anyone else's for that matter.

As we have seen in the preceding pages, Hemingway had good reason to complain about some of the films based on his work. But since he consistently chose to dismiss virtually every film made from his work with a derogatory quip —whether he had seen all of it or not—one suspects that he somehow felt required to knock almost any movie adaptation of his work in order to preserve his literary status. It was unnecessary for him to do this, however, since his literary reputation and that of his work was not affected one way or another by any film made from his fiction.

It was less than fair of him to mention his outrage at the preliminary script of *The Sun Also Rises* but never to divulge that King and Viertel personally took the final revised shooting script to him for his comments and suggestions aboard the *Ile de France*. Furthermore, his criticism of a film of one of his works, even when meant seriously, could be merely captious. He expressed concern, for example, that audiences would detect that the fiesta scenes in *Sun* were shot not in Spain but in Mexico because the extras "looked" Mexican and not Spanish.

Henry King's explanation for going to Mexico rather than to Spain for location work seems reasonable: "I visited Pamplona to see what it would be like at the time of year we were scheduled to shoot there, and it was four feet deep in snow! I told Zanuck that, since we already had second unit footage of a bullfight which was shot in Spain, we could do the rest in a town in Mexico called Morelia. As things turned out, the city officials in Morelia allowed me to paint the interior of their bullring to match the colors of the bullring in Pamplona where some of the second unit footage had already been done. We used long shots of the bullfight in Pamplona and intercut it with shots of the bullfight which we staged in Morelia especially for the movie."

King had originally planned to use a bona fide bullfighter to play the part of Romero, so that it would be clear that the same individual who was enacting Romero in the dramatic scenes of the picture was in actual fact also fighting the bulls in the arena. In this way King could lend a more authentic flavor to the bullfighting sequences by avoiding the traditional Hollywood dodge of alternating close-ups of the face of the actor who is supposedly doing the bullfighting with long shots of the stand-in who is actually doing so.

"I tested one up-and-coming Mexican bullfighter and he was my choice for Romero," King recalled. "I was going to bring him to the United States and teach him English and acting for three months. But Zanuck said that he looked more like a waiter than a bullfighter, and cast a young actor named Bob Evans instead." Evans was not convincing as a Spanish bullfighter, and in addition proved uncooperative in working with Miguel Delgado, who was shooting the second unit material on the bullfight in the arena.

"My man was doubling for Evans in the bullfighting scenes," said King; "and Zanuck wanted to use him to replace Evans altogether after he saw the rushes of the arena sequences. But by then it was too late to train the Mexican bullfighter in both English and in acting as I had wanted to do in the first place. So we had to stick with Evans. He went on to be an excellent producer, but he was never much of an actor."

The Sun Also Rises may not be the best of the Hemingway movies, but it is certainly the most underrated. In it King assembled an incomparable cast of first-rate actors, with Gardner and Flynn in particular giving permanent life to the lost generation on the screen in a pair of performances which rank among their best. In addition, the film is fairly faithful to the novel, despite some departures from the text; and Hemingway himself in fact had more to do with bringing the script into line with his book than he was ever publicly prepared to admit. In the last analysis, his supercilious put-down of the film reveals more about his studied conde-scension to the movie medium than it does about the worth of the picture.

Henry King never lost his lasting appreciation for Hemingway's fiction. "Hemingway," he told me at the conclusion of our interview, "is a much deeper writer than people give him credit for. He makes every word count and, as I have often said, if you don't read every line carefully you will miss the nuances. He has a beautiful style, as spare and methodical as a first-class prizefighter."

Hemingway's style was more in evidence in the script for *The Old Man and the Sea* than in any other film adaptation of his work, for his own narration and dialogue were used almost exclusively in the film. He also personally supervised the script written by Peter Viertel and served as technical adviser on the film, giving the movie a unique distinction among the motion pictures drawn from his fiction. "The one he wanted made most of all was *Old Man and the Sea*," says Peter Viertel; "and even that didn't work out very well, although the text was his."[23] Let us find out why.

8
The Undefeated:
The Old Man and the Sea (1958) and *Islands in the Stream* (1977)

AFTER HEMINGWAY RETURNED FROM HIS stint as a war correspondent for *Collier's* magazine during World War II, he sometimes jokingly referred to himself as Old Ernie Hemorrhoid, the poor man's Pyle. But he was quite serious when he announced that he had gathered enough material to compose a three-volume novel about the war that would outclass his last published novel, *For Whom the Bell Tolls*, which had appeared in 1940. The new novel would devote separate volumes to the war on sea, on land, and in the air. The first volume, *The Sea*, was to be set in the early days of the war. It would in turn be divided into three sections: "The Sea When Young," "The Sea When Absent," and "The Sea in Being."

The land and air volumes of Hemingway's war trilogy, which were slated to treat the later phases of the war, never got written at all—though Hemingway would draw on what he knew of the land war as background material for his 1950 novel about a dying veteran, *Across the River and Into the Trees*.

However, by 1947 he had completed a preliminary draft of the first portion of the sea novel, "The Sea When Young," tentatively retitled "The Island and the Stream"; then he laid aside the project to write *Across the River*. By the spring of 1951 he had finished the second segment, "The Sea When Absent," and a third episode called "The Sea Chase." It had not been in his original plan at all, and he inserted it in his design just before "The Sea in Being." The first three parts of the novel all dealt with Thomas Hudson, an American artist living in Cuba at the outbreak of the war, who was as obviously based on Hemingway himself as any hero the author had ever created.

"The Sea in Being," written in early 1951, was now the fourth episode of the sea novel. Although it had been conceived from the start as a thematic coda to the preceding incidents about Thomas Hudson, it did not in fact deal with Hudson at all, but with an aging Cuban fisherman whose real story the novelist had been told. Hemingway had first narrated the old man's encounter with a great marlin in an essay written for *Esquire* back in 1935; fifteen years later he now fictionalized the episode as the fourth and final part of the sea novel.

Because the essential plot of the story had been simmering in his imagination so long, and because of his accumulated experience as a writer over a quarter of a century, the story seemed to write itself and required little revision. Hemingway tentatively retitled the work "The Old and the Young," but finally chose to call it "The Old Man and the Sea."

As for the Thomas Hudson material, because he had not sufficiently polished the text or inserted the missing transitional passages needed to unify the episodes into a coherent and unified piece of fiction, Hemingway never felt that it was ready for publication. (The Thomas Hudson episodes were published by Hemingway's widow in 1970 as a separate book under the title *Islands in the Stream*.) Thoroughly convinced of the high quality of the fourth part of the sea novel, however,

Hemingway decided that it could stand alone. In 1952, he therefore published it separately as the novella *The Old Man and the Sea*. It won him his only Pulitzer Prize (1953) and certainly clinched his winning the Nobel Prize in 1954.

As Hemingway outlined the story of the old man and the marlin in his *Esquire* article, the aged fisherman landed the giant fish after wrestling with it for two days and two nights, only to have it ravaged by a school of sharks before he could tow it back to shore (its gigantic size prohibited his carrying it inside his flimsy little skiff). Hemingway reported in *Esquire* that the old man was a physical and emotional wreck as a result of his ordeal, and that he was sobbing hopelessly "and half crazy from his loss" when some other fisherman picked him up and brought him back to land.[1]

However, Santiago, Hemingway's ancient mariner in the novella, completely transcends the real-life model on which he was based. His stoic endurance and courage in battling the marlin and the sharks make him a supreme code hero. Furthermore, he exhibits a sense of resignation and a dignity in apparent defeat that qualifies him in religious terms as a Christ figure, at one with the apparent failure of Calvary. As Frederic Henry says in *A Farewell to Arms*, it is in reconciling one's self to suffering and loss that one becomes truly Christian: "I don't mean technically Christian. I mean like Our Lord."[2]

It has been said that the best steel will break but it will not bend, an aphorism that recalls Santiago's personal testament to the indomitability of the human spirit: "A man can be destroyed but not defeated."[3] Defeat implies that one succumbs to one's fate without putting up a fight, whereas an authentic code hero like Santiago goes down swinging; and that is no defeat. In Hemingway's world, what really counts in the last analysis is not winning or losing but playing the game by the rules. When Santiago, bloodied but unbowed, returns home at the end of the novella he says that something inside him is broken; whatever it is, we know that it is certainly not his spirit, for that he has preserved completely unimpaired.

By participating vicariously in the old man's experiences, the boy Manolo, who knows the old man so well, achieves as an apprentice hero the same kind of initiation into the life-and-death struggle of existence vouchsafed Nick Adams before him in "Indian Camp."

In writing the novella Hemingway felt that he had, like Santiago, gone "way past what I thought I could do." He repeated this sentiment in his Nobel Prize acceptance speech, saying that a writer must try each time that he attempts to write a book to surpass his previous achievements; and he is therefore "driven out past where he can go, out to where no one can help him."

William Faulkner called *The Old Man and the Sea* Hemingway's best because "this time he discovered God, a Creator," who made and loved and pitied all of the characters in the story, even the sharks which were driven by instinct to rob the old man of his marlin. "Praise God," Faulkner concluded, "that whatever made and loves and pities Hemingway and me kept him from touching it any further."

Although Hemingway's personal sense of rivalry with Faulkner had poisoned his attitude toward his fellow novelist and had led him to convince himself that Faulkner was a "no-good son-of-a-bitch,"[4] Faulkner was right on target in divining that the stark, spare simplicity of the novella was its greatest virtue. Surely any film version that was derived from the novella would have to be characterized by the same kind of simplicity that characterized the novella, if it were to claim any degree of fidelity to Hemingway's book.

Since Hemingway's own agent, Leland Hayward, had offered to produce the film adaptation of *The Old Man and the Sea* and to sign on Hemingway both to supervise the script and to act as technical adviser on the picture, there seemed to be no reason why a faithful movie version of the novella could not be forthcoming.

Hayward and Hemingway were contemplating a semi-documentary approach to filming the novella, employing, as Hemingway put it, "local people on a local ocean with a local boat,"[5] with a narrator reading appropriate passages of the text on the sound track. Hayward secured the services of Spencer Tracy as narrator; and the actor expressed his willingness from the start to do a cross-country reading tour of *The Old Man and the Sea* as promotion for the film and as a warm-up for his delivering the movie's narration. Hemingway, Hayward, and Tracy then formed a partnership to make the film as an independent production.

The director who first came to mind was Vittorio De Sica, noted for the unvarnished realism of such postwar Italian films as *The Bicycle Thief* (1949). But the triad eventually

Spencer Tracy is virtually the entire cast of *The Old Man and the Sea* (1958). Shooting began on location in the waters off the Cuban coast under Hemingway's personal supervision as technical adviser. But after months of well-publicized production troubles the film was finished, against Hemingway's wishes, back in Hollywood in the studio tank. (The Museum of Modern Art/Film Stills Archive)

settled on Fred Zinnemann who had impressed Tracy when he directed the actor in *The Seventh Cross* (1944), and who had just directed the brilliant *High Noon*. In addition, Zinnemann had made a semidocumentary film about Mexican fishermen called *The Wave* (1935), which he had shot on location in Mexico in a simple, straightforward, realistic style with nonprofessional actors. This was exactly the format that Hayward and Hemingway had in mind for *The Old Man and the Sea;* Zinnemann was evidently much in sympathy with the way that they wanted the picture made.

Warner Brothers, which was to finance and distribute the film, however, demanded that Tracy play the title role of Santiago as well as narrate the film, in order to increase the film's box-office potential. Hayward and Hemingway complied with this stipulation; and Tracy in turn promised to lose weight in order to look more convincing in the part (a promise which in fact he did not keep, much to Hemingway's subsequent disappointment).

Tracy, Hemingway, and Hayward finalized arrangements for the film in the spring of 1953. Hemingway would receive $150,000 for the screen rights of the novella and an additional $75,000 for acting as technical adviser on the picture, plus an eventual percentage of the profits. Because of Tracy's prior film commitments, however, the actor could not undertake the reading tour and also could not begin shooting the picture for another three years.

Accordingly, it was not until the summer of 1955 that Peter Viertel and Leland Hayward flew to Hemingway's home in Cuba, Finca Vigía, for script conferences with the novelist. Viertel has since revealed that Hemingway insisted somewhat eccentrically that Viertel get himself into the proper mood to write the screenplay by submitting to a curious preliminary regimen calculated to make the screenwriter share Santiago's experiences as much as possible. Hemingway's checklist included Viertel's spending the night in a stifling, insect-ridden shack; attempting to catch a marlin on his own; and being set adrift offshore in a dinghy for a couple of hours under a punishing sun. Eventually, Hemingway was satisfied that Viertel was ready to write a screenplay that would be an authentic transcription of his short novel.

The following note appears at the beginning of the screenplay and is emblematic of the faithfulness of the script to its literary source. "Please remember that the book itself is the basis of this film," it reads, "and that its use in conjunction with this continuity is essential." The thematic content as well as the plotline of the novella was strictly adhered to in the screenplay. Hence most of the religious symbolism in the story is transferred virtually intact to the film script.

For example, Santiago's status as a Christ figure is explicitly confirmed in the screenplay by the image of him shouldering the mast of his boat in order to carry it back to his shack after he returns from sea and falling several times beneath its weight on the way up the hill to his home. Some critics of both film and book have found the religious imagery fairly heavy-handed; it cannot be denied, however, that it underscores the overarching humanistic theme of the book: sometimes losing is ultimately the only way to win. Though in both the book and the film Santiago wonders if he forfeited the marlin to the sharks by chasing it too long and too far, we implicitly infer that, like the leopard scaling the heights of Mt. Kilimanjaro, Santiago's dogged pursuit of his prize demonstrates once again that one's reach must exceed one's grasp, or what's a heaven for?

Viertel and Hayward wanted to include several short sequences in the screenplay that would serve to ward off the potential tedium which could well result from the bulk of the movie taking place in a small skiff in midocean. Among them were a prologue in which the impecunious Santiago fruitlessly looks for work in Havana before desperately returning to his fishing boat in the hope that his prevailing run of bad luck will change, and a flashback which would depict a younger Santiago courting his wife, now deceased. Hemingway steadfastly vetoed these and other ideas for opening up the screenplay of his novella on the assumption that scenes that he had not created for his book in the first place could only prove to be excess baggage in the screenplay.

Since Hemingway had script approval, his decision in this and other matters regarding the screenplay were scrupulously adhered to. But as things turned out Viertel and Hayward had been absolutely right in wanting to add these few extra scenes, which were in fact completely in keeping with the spirit of the work as a whole. The one flashback that is included in the film—because it was already in the novella—works very well. In order to shore up his confidence about conquering the marlin, Santiago recalls how he bested an opponent in a handwrestling contest. The movie could have used more brief sequences of this kind, for without them the final film wound up with some undeniably dull passages in its central section, during which the viewer must watch Tracy emoting all by himself in a small boat in the middle of the open sea.

With the script fairly well in shape by the end of the summer of 1955, a second unit crew arrived in Cuba to shoot preliminary fishing footage in September of that year. Hurricanes discouraged the really big marlin from cruising in the Gulf Stream near the Cuban coast, and the attendant dark skies and rainy weather created conditions totally unfavorable for color photography. When Zinnemann, Hayward, and Tracy all arrived to begin filming in earnest the following spring everyone agreed, therefore, that the material shot the previous September should be scrapped.

Hemingway volunteered to capture a prize marlin for the movie cameras, and mounted an expedition to do so. "To try and film a really big marlin of one thousand pounds or more," Mary Hemingway says, "we went to Peru and fished for a month off Cabo Blanco: Ernest and Elicín Argüelles, a Cuban sports-fishing friend of ours on the fishing boat; and I, as translator for the Peruvian crew, on the camera boat," since the camera operator and his two assistants from Hollywood knew no Spanish. "We fished every day for a month in those heavy seas without luck."[6]

"We fished for thirty-two days from early morning until it was too late to photograph," Hemingway has written. "The marlin were large and did not fight as the fish off Cuba do. But their weight and bulk in the heavy seas made it hard to work; and a fish that you could bring to gaff in eight or twelve minutes you would let run again, holding him always in close camera range," so that the second unit film crew could get the best shots that they could of the big fish.[7] Yet, withal, Hemingway and company did not land a marlin spectacular enough to stand in for Santiago's gigantic catch; and Hayward ordered the Peruvian fishing expedition to strike their colors and return to base.

Difficulties of this kind dogged the production on every side. For one thing, Hemingway was severely disappointed that Tracy had not bothered either to perfect a Spanish accent or to lose weight in order to make himself more like Santiago. "Ernest was very fond of Fred Zinnemann, who came down to Cuba to film the beginning of *The Old Man and the Sea*," Mary Hemingway recalls, "but could not like the casting of Spencer Tracy (although they were personal friends) in the role of Santiago. 'Him with his big fat feet,' Ernest said. And of course Tracy, with all of his talent, could not look like a thin old Cuban fisherman."[8]

To make matters worse, Zinnemann resigned from the picture; he was replaced by John Sturges, whom Tracy recommended as a result of working with him on *Bad Day at Black Rock* two years earlier. There are several conflicting reports as to why Zinnemann resigned his directorial duties. Tracy claimed that Zinnemann's disagreements were with Hayward and not with him; and one rumor had it that Zinnemann left the picture after Jack Warner phoned him from Hollywood to complain about some early rushes. Queried about this, Zinnemann replied, "I can assure you that, while it is true that I quit *The Old Man and the Sea*, it had nothing to do with Jack Warner's viewing the rushes."[9]

In conversation with me, Zinnemann noted that a primary reason for his resignation from the production was that the turbulent Gulf Stream waters around Cuba made it frustratingly difficult to take boatloads of camera equipment out in the water and photograph Tracy in his skiff. Zinnemann became increasingly convinced that the film could not be finished under these conditions, but he could not persuade studio officials back in Hollywood of this fact. After he left the film, however, the front office decided to allow Sturges to continue shooting in the more benign waters around the Hawaiian islands. "Fred had shot about eight minutes of film," says Sturges, "and we used about four of those minutes in the picture."[10]

By this time, however, Warner stockholders were complaining that the production was going substantially beyond its $2,000,000 budget; Warner Brothers decided to shut down production in Hawaii and to move the entire company back to the studios in Burbank, California. Already thoroughly disillusioned with moviemaking in general and shooting *The Old Man and the Sea* in particular, Hemingway was heartbroken when the film was finished with a foam-rubber fish in the studio tank. "It took something out of Ernest when that decision was made," writes his younger brother Leicester.[11]

The novelist had said that he had tried to write a story about a real old man, a real sea, and a real fish; "and if I made them good and true they would mean many things."[12] But the film version was finishing up with an inauthentic Santiago, an artificial ocean, and a phony fish. Expressing his feelings about the film, Ernest Hemingway noted that after spending months on the script and photography of a motion picture taken from a "book that you believed in and loved, you know that now you will never again interrupt the work that you were born and trained to do until you die."[13]

Ernest and Mary Hemingway did not follow the production to Hollywood, but each is visible in one of the scenes shot in Cuba. Ernest can be seen sporting a checkered shirt as one of the onlookers in the flashback sequence of the handwrestling contest which Santiago had won as a younger man; and Mary appears among the American tourists in the closing moments of the film.

Shooting resumed in Hollywood in the fall of 1957, after Tracy had fulfilled still another film commitment in the interim. "This picture is becoming my life's work," he commented at the time. "By now there isn't a chance to make all the money we will spend, so we're just concentrating on making it worthwhile."[14]

James Wong Howe, the veteran cinematographer in charge of photographing the film, must also have felt that the movie was becoming his life's work too; his patience and ingenuity were taxed to the limit during the prolonged period that the film was in production as he faced big problems and small. At one point John Sturges wanted a bird to come down and land on the hand of the old fisherman while he sat in his little fishing boat. "I didn't want to have to coax the bird all day to fly down from its perch out of camera range into the boat," Howe explained. "So I weighted down its feathers with beebee shot, and it flew down into the boat by Tracy's hand almost immediately. Then Tracy moved his hand over toward the bird slightly, and it hopped right onto his hand. This shows how much luck there is involved in filmmaking. It could have taken hours to get that bird to hop onto Tracy's hand." With everything else going wrong, at least the bird was cooperative.

The Old Man and the Sea was noteworthy for Howe's expert location photography. Howe "conjured beautiful images of the sea and sky," says critic Gordon Gow, "of boats cutting through the surf when the Old Man dreamed of youthful days in Africa, and of the gathering of fishermen with furled sails and lanterns to light their way to the harbor in the dark before dawn."[15]

It was surely no fault of Howe's that John Sturges had to declare when the picture was completed that it was "technically the sloppiest picture I have ever made."[16] In editing the film, Sturges, himself a former editor, had laboriously but unsuccessfully tried to match the location footage, the studio footage, and some shots taken by fisherman Alfred Glassell, who had recently caught the biggest marlin on record. This last material, which Glassell had made available for use in the film, had been photographed on 16mm film in black and white; hence only a few long shots of his marlin, tinted to simulate the color photography of the rest of the movie as nearly as possible, could be used.

Despite the best efforts of Sturges and of his editor, Arthur Schmidt, it was simply impossible to mesh footage photographed under such drastically different circumstances into a visually integrated whole. "In view of all of the technical problems and the process work," Gow writes in his perceptive treatment of this film, "there was the occasional fuzz, the odd and obvious outline that divorced the Old Man's hand from the authentic background of the sea" when a studio close-up of Tracy's hand was superimposed on a location shot of the ocean.

Raising another issue, the use in the film of such large chunks of Hemingway's original narration, Gow cites Sturges on his reasons for doing so: "We put the words against a background that seemed commensurate with them. We used them simply to hear them: to let Spence say them. It seemed to me that what happened on the screen wasn't as powerful as what was said—literally the words."[17]

Sturges experimented with deleting some of the spoken commentary; in the end, however, he decided that since there was little opportunity for dialogue all the commentary was needed to help convey to the viewer the inner thoughts and emotions not only of the Old Man but also of the boy. The commentary was made doubly necessary by the fact that the unlettered Santiago and Manolin could in any case hardly have been sufficiently articulate to give adequate expression to the nuances of their thoughts and feelings. The narrator had to do this for the viewer.

The problem that arises from this liberal use of narration on the sound track is that at times it leads to a certain redundancy, whereby the audience is simultaneously told and shown the same thing. "The boy saw the Old Man's hands and he started to cry," the narrator tells us, voice-over; and we see tears in the lad's eyes as he looks at the Old Man's battered hands after Santiago returns from his fishing trip. At such times the commentary is totally unnecessary, since the situation described on the sound track is obvious from the images on the screen. Consequently, at times Sturges seems to be illustrating Hemingway's prose as one would do in a slide lecture, rather than attempting to convert his words into visual images that should stand on their own.

Tracy employs his natural voice to read the narration, and does so in a sonorous yet mellow manner which is well nigh impeccable. But the wavering, almost nondescript accent in which Tracy speaks Santiago's lines, plus his obvious girth, combine to handicap the actor in giving a convincing protrayal as an old Cuban fisherman. Nevertheless, his performance gradually grows on the filmgoer, for he enacts the role with conviction and invests it with compassion. When at long last the film was released in 1958, Tracy received widespread plaudits for bringing off the entire film virtually singlehanded, since for much of the movie's running time he was the only actor on the screen.

For once Hemingway sat through a film made from his fiction. When the picture was over, he declared that he was numb and irritably characterized Tracy's performance as that of a "fat, very rich actor playing a fisherman."[18] Some months earlier he had told newsman Denne Petitclerc that he continued to be nettled about what he considered to be Tracy's lack of cooperation during the shooting of *Old Man:* "The thing about stars is they always seem like nice guys until

the movie starts. Then the cameras roll and Tracy is suddenly
the big movie star with the movie star temper. Nobody could
go near him or tell him anything."[19]

Tracy was nominated for an Academy Award, but the
film's only Oscar went to Dimitri Tiomkin for his score—a
curious choice since Tiomkin's somewhat inflated musical
background seemed at times to be at odds with the spare
simplicity of the rest of the movie. In general reviewers
admired the picture, but complained that the swollen budget
—it had more than doubled by the time the movie was
finished because of the well-publicized troubles during the
overdrawn location period—was not sufficiently evident on
the screen. This is because the location footage ultimately
accounted for a mere one-tenth of the film's final print; the
bulk of the picture's usable footage had been shot in the studio
tank. As a result, the most expensive Hemingway film ever
made wound up looking like a low-budget picture.

The film was fated to be financial disaster (although it has
since attracted a respectable audience on network TV); and
Hemingway's final comment on the whole venture was to
moan, "No picture with a fucking rubber fish ever made a
dime."[20] (This remark was made, of course, before the era of
Jaws.)

Despite his diatribes against the film adaptations of his
fiction, Hemingway never seemed to lose hope that a viable
film could be made from his fiction. "I got one piece, a long
book, that would make a pretty good movie," he confided to
Denne Petitclerc; however, he added that it would have to be
revised substantially before it was ready for publication,
much less for filming.[21] The revision of the work in question,
the three Thomas Hudson episodes of the sea novel, was
never completed—perhaps because Hemingway found the
work so intimately autobiographical that the task proved
increasingly too difficult and delicate.

Like Hemingway, the hero of the posthumously published *Islands in the Stream* is a divorcé with three growing sons from his two previous marriages and an expatriate American living in the Caribbean. The closest parallel between Hudson and Hemingway revolves around an incident which dates from the early days of World War II when Hemingway outfitted his fishing launch, the *Pilar*, with a small arsenal and patrolled the Cuban coast in search of Nazi U-boats. Hemingway and his loyal crew never captured a single German submarine, but Thomas Hudson locates a sunken Nazi sub and is killed in an exchange of gunfire with the survivors of the crew.

Thomas Hudson is the code hero of the novel while his three sons, whom he tries to influence for the better, make up a kind of collective apprentice hero. But Hudson, with his sullen sense of commitment to duty mingled with a subconscious death wish, belongs to the second echelon of Hemingway code heroes. And when one recalls that Hemingway's original concept for his four-part sea novel was to place *The Old Man and the Sea* after the three Thomas Hudson episodes as a thematic coda, it is possible to see the admirable Santiago as having attained a moral stature for which Hudson was still striving when his life was halted by an enemy bullet. In this way *Islands in the Stream* and *The Old Man and the Sea* can be seen to complement each other nicely.

Thomas Hudson is nevertheless an interesting character on his own, and his story seemed to Denne Petitclerc to be ripe for screen treatment when he read the book more than a decade after Hemingway had first mentioned it to him. Having become a scriptwriter, Petitclerc secured from Mary Hemingway permission to write a screenplay based on *Islands in the Stream*. Peter Bart and Max Palevsky agreed to produce it as a motion picture when he finished the script more than two years later.

Petitclerc revised his script with the help of director Franklin Schaffner and star Steve McQueen. It was McQueen who suggested that the death of Thomas Hudson's oldest son, Tom, Jr., in World War II be retained in the film, but not the demise of his two younger sons, David and Andrew, in an auto accident; the death of all three sons, McQueen argued, would stretch the viewer's credulity (as it does the reader's) and might also push the film over the line from pathos to bathos.

In the wake of all of this reworking of the script in story conferences, Petitclerc managed to tighten the rambling plot of the novel and to supply the transitions needed to link one episode to the next. In this way he came up with a well-honed screen story that was to some degree more unified than the loosely constructed first-draft novel from which it was drawn.

As things turned out, McQueen had to depart to fulfill an overlapping contractual commitment on another film, and Schaffner sent the script to George C. Scott, whom he had directed in his Oscar-winning performance in *Patton* a few years earlier. Scott replied: "Don't change a word. When do we start?" Paramount agreed to distribute the film, and Schaffner and his associates set out for the Hawaiian island of Kauai to do location work. This island was chosen, says Bart, because "the structures were amazingly 1940's, the climate was perfect, the political and social environment benign, and its waters were generally hospitable."[22] In short, Schaffner and his cast and crew were assured that they were going to be able to avoid the myriad location problems that had all but sunk the production of *Old Man and the Sea.*

The film of *Islands in the Stream* is divided, like the book, into three parts. The centerpiece of the first segment, "The Boys," is the attempt of David (Michael Wixted) to land a hammerhead swordfish, and might in turn be labeled "The Young Man and the Sea," since it parallels Santiago's bout with the marlin. In this sequence Hudson functions as a code hero in that he tries to use the incident to help David and his brothers learn about life from the experience. When David

Eddy (David Hemmings), David (Michael Wixted), Thomas Hudson (George C. Scott), and Andrew (Brad Savage) in Franklin Schaffner's *Islands in the Stream* (1977). This scene might be termed "The Young Man and the Sea." Scott was deliberately made up to look like Hemingway, who had in fact modeled the character of Hudson on himself. (The Museum of Modern Art/Film Stills Archive)

loses the hammerhead, Hudson explains to the boys that David has been toughened by manfully meeting the challenge in a way that will help him to face other demanding experiences in later life.

The second segment of the film, "The Woman," is built around the visit of Hudson's first wife, Audrey (Claire Bloom), whom he still loves, some time after the departure of his sons. This portion of the movie is climaxed by the revelation that their son, Tom, Jr., has been killed in the war and ends with Hudson's realization, after she departs, that he is bereft not only of a beloved son but of the lad's mother as well; for with Tom's death the last link between Audrey and him has been severed; and consequently the last hope of any reconciliation with her is gone.

In the final portion of the film, "The Journey," Hudson decides to help smuggle Jewish refugees into Cuba as one way of recklessly distracting himself from his loneliness and grief. In the movie, therefore, Hudson is shot while being pursued by the Cuban coast guard, rather than while he is pursuing Nazi sailors, as in the book. But the upshot is the same, and the film's fast-paced finale ends with Hudson dying on the deck of his fishing launch as he succumbs to his bullet wounds.

Besides paring down the number of characters and incidents used in the film in order to clarify the overall logic of the story line, the filmmakers have also made other efforts to connect the book's three sections more solidly. One such linking device used in the movie is the planting of hints in the earlier stages of the film of incidents that will occur later. For example, in the movie Hudson and his sons discover the corpse of a Nazi sailor on the shore near his home; and this serves to foreshadow the eventual involvement of both Thomas Hudson and his son Tom in the war that will claim their lives. Hudson reflects a sense of foreboding as he murmurs, while contemplating the dead German, "I pray for a short war."

Film critic Brendan Gill seems to overstate his case considerably when he writes that "the insuperable defect of *Islands* is that it is not one movie but two. The first movie has to do with a middle-aged man's love for his three growing sons; the second movie has to do with rescuing some refugees from the Nazis during the Second World War."[23]

While it is true that the movie lacks the strong connective tissue between its episodes which one normally finds in a motion picture (as evidenced by the fact that the movie, like the book, is clearly divided into three "acts," each introduced by a title), it is also true that the plot of the picture is much more cohesive than that of the book on which it is based because of the cross-references between various events which the filmmakers have introduced into the screenplay through the use of foreshadowing and other narrative devices. Though critic Christopher Porterfield thought that the film tended at times to oversimplify Hemingway's book, he nonetheless recognized that the way in which the makers of *Islands* distilled Hemingway's story was a real asset to the movie, shearing away as they did "reams of embarrassingly arch, blustery" incidents "and mannered barroom colloquies."[24]

The moviemakers also have lent additional strength and resonance to their version of Hemingway's first-draft novel by borrowing bits of dialogue from other Hemingway works. Thomas Hudson's dying reflections were actually penned by Hemingway for Robert Jordan at the end of *For Whom the Bell Tolls*, but they fit perfectly into the spirit of the final scene of *Islands*: "I've had a lot of luck to have had such a good life," Hudson reflects. "I wish there was some way to pass on what I've learned. I was learning fast there at the end."[25]

Thomas Hudson has learned in his final encounters with Audrey and his sons, and with close companions like Eddie (David Hemmings), that no man need be an island in the stream of humanity if he but realizes that he is loved and learns to return that love in kind. But for Thomas Hudson it is already too late to profit by this new-found insight since his life is now over. His friend Joseph sobs as Hudson's life ebbs away, "I love you, you son-of-a-bitch; you never understand about anyone loving you."[26]

George C. Scott brilliantly projected the complex character of Thomas Hudson in the film. In order to underline the resemblances between Ernest Hemingway's personality and past history and that of Thomas Hudson, Scott was made up to look like the middle-aged Hemingway, complete with a salt-and-pepper beard turning white. But unlike his fictional creation, Ernest Hemingway did not perish at the hands of others. Hemingway's death wish was fulfilled when he died by his own hand in his own home, less than three weeks before his sixty-second birthday.

9
Epilogue: Across the Selznick and into the Zanuck

THE GUNSHOT WITH WHICH ERNEST Hemingway terminated his life, as Carlos Baker remarks in the essay which serves as the foreword to this book, was heard round the world, as tributes and memorials were rushed into print in all parts of the globe. Death came for one of America's most celebrated writers on a Sunday morning in July 1961, when his third attempt at suicide during his last, long illness proved successful.

In the preceding months his health, both physical and mental, had rapidly deteriorated. He had spent several weeks at the Mayo clinic in Rochester, Minnesota, where he underwent various forms of treatment, including electroshock therapy to alleviate his severe depression. After he was released a second time from the clinic, he returned home to Ketchum, Idaho, on Friday, June 30, 1961. At 7 A.M. the following Sunday he picked up his favorite gun, a double-barreled, twelve-gauge shotgun inlaid with silver. Taking careful aim at his own forehead, he pulled both triggers and blasted away most of his head.

Hemingway had been preoccupied with suicide one way or another most of his life. When he was wounded in Italy during World War I, he felt at first as if his life had slipped away from his body, "like you'd pull a silk handkerchief out of a pocket by one corner," and then returned.[1] The thought occurred to him that he should end his life there and then since, as he later explained in a letter to his father: "How much better to die in all the happy period of undisillusioned youth, to go out in a blaze of light, than to have your body worn out and old, and illusions shattered."[2]

Both the sender and the receiver of that letter were one day to commit suicide. That his father's suicide haunted Hemingway is evidenced by the veiled references to it in the Nick Adams story "Fathers and Sons" and in *For Whom the Bell Tolls*. He believed, as Anthony Burgess has noted, that "grace must always be maintained under pressure, no matter how killing the pressure. He was bitterly ashamed of what his father had done."[3]

By the time Ernest Hemingway followed his father's example, he was indeed a worn-out old man with all of his illusions shattered. He had become convinced, for example, that like the hero of "The Snows of Kilimanjaro" he would never fulfill his talent as a writer to the degree that he had hoped; hence he felt that he had nothing left to live for. That his suicide was contrary both to the code to which he subscribed in his fiction and to the tenets of his religious faith, however, is a clear indication that he was not in his right mind when he became the author of his own destruction.

Although Hemingway had never publicized his personal beliefs because he did not want to be characterized as a "Catholic author" writing only for his co-religionists, he considered himself a Roman Catholic from the night in 1918 when an Italian army chaplain, Don Giuseppi Bianchi, received him into the Church while he was awaiting surgery for his wounded leg in the field hospital. Both Hemingway and Don Giuseppi thought that he might be dying; and when the priest offered to baptize him as a Catholic he consented, as he explained afterward, "just in case they were right."[4]

Throughout the rest of his life Hemingway continued to believe that "they were right." He attended Sunday Mass regularly wherever he was, subscribed to a magazine about the apostolic work of the Jesuit order, and confided to fellow convert Gary Cooper that he firmly "believed in belief." He confessed on another occasion that he had more faith in his religious convictions than he had understanding of them, but added that he always tried to live a good life in the Church and was happy for it. Hemingway, moreover, generously presented his Nobel Prize gold medal to the shrine of the Blessed Virgin at Santiago de Cuba.[5]

Hotchner remembers the piety which Hemingway displayed when they visited a cathedral together in Spain in 1954. After Hemingway unobtrusively knelt in silent prayer at a side altar for several minutes, he murmured as they descended the cathedral steps, "Sometimes I wish I were a better Catholic."[6] That he somehow held on to his chosen religious faith to the end of his life, even in the face of periods of serious mental illness, is evidenced by the fact that during his second stay at the Mayo Clinic he said to the hospital chaplain, Father Cyril Therres, "Father, I would be very pleased to have you bless me."

Nevertheless, because as Hemingway himself admitted, "many things have happened about divorces and remarriages,"[7] he could not be accorded a Catholic funeral mass. But this circumstance did not preclude a Catholic priest's officiating at the graveside burial service. Nor was his suicide an impediment to Catholic burial since it was manifestly not the act of a sane man. Hemingway's behavior after leaving the Mayo Clinic the second time confirmed Mary Hemingway's fear that he had charmed his doctors into releasing him prematurely. His suspicions about being stalked by the FBI and other paranoid fantasies persisted after they returned to Ketchum and were a painfully clear indication that Hemingway was emotionally disturbed when he took his life.

Father Robert Waldmann, pastor of Our Lady of the Snows Catholic church in Ketchum, presided at the cemetery burial rites. Perhaps a quotation from one of the Nick Adams stories, "The Big Two-Hearted River," would also have been appropriate for the occasion: "He felt he had left everything behind him, the need for thinking, the need to write, other needs. It was all back of him. . . . Now it was done."[8]

Hemingway's achievement as a major American writer is generally recognized. But to what extent was the impact of Hemingway's fiction transferred to the films which were adapted from it? Hemingway himself was not the best judge of this. He generally tended to underestimate the quality of these films, principally because he never really grasped the fundamental differences between film and fiction as two separate artistic media. He could never accept the inescapable fact that expansion or compression of his material would inevitably be necessary in order to accommodate one of his short stories or novels to the very different format of an essentially visual medium.

Aaron Hotchner recalls showing Hemingway the script of a TV adaptation which he had done of one of the novelist's short stories. The next day, Hemingway returned the script to him with all of the dialogue passages in it carefully altered to bring them into verbatim conformity with the printed text of the original short story. Such literal fidelity to a literary source is rarely if ever possible when a work is adapted to the screen, and can hardly be the criterion by which an adaptation is judged.

It cannot be too often emphasized that the faithful film adaption must preserve the spirit and overall thrust of the original work, regardless of the superficial liberties taken with the plot and dialogue of the parent work in retooling it for the screen. In point of fact, the complex thematic structure of the

Hemingway code as found in his fiction is implicitly present in varying degrees in most of the motion pictures based on his work.

As an artist, he had undeniably justifiable complaints about certain aspects of the films drawn from his fiction; and he certainly had every right to be disgruntled about the way that the uncompromising endings of his works were sometimes tampered with for commercial considerations. He could hardly have been expected to be happy with the ending of the film of "The Snows of Kilimanjaro," in which the hero survives the death which Hemingway as author clearly meant to be inevitable. Concerning the movie's ending he could only stoically note: "We must look on that as a very minor change, don't you think?"

He went on to speculate in the same conversation with Aaron Hotchner about a possible Hollywood version of his 1950 novel *Across the River and into the Trees*, in which the tired old soldier would not expire in the back seat of his car on the outskirts of Venice, but would hike back to town, "walk down the middle of the Grand Canal, . . . and into Harry's bar dry-shod." The film, he concluded, could be entitled *Across the Selznick and into the Zanuck*, after the two producers he disliked the most.

In fact, a film version of *Across the River and into the Trees* had been in the works for years. Hemingway had agreed to sell the movie rights to his old friend Gary Cooper when the actor showed interest in playing the lead role of Colonel Cantwell. "You'd just be playing Robert Jordan ten years later," Hemingway said to Cooper enthusiastically.[9] As mentioned earlier, Hemingway's hope that a good movie could be made from one of his fictional works never seemed to dim, notwithstanding his past disappointment with Hollywood.

Though Cooper did not live to make the movie, John Huston became interested in filming the novel in 1975. Hopes were high among Hemingway buffs for a reputable screen version of the novel since Huston had co-authored the screenplay of the 1946 *Killers.* "I want my pictures to have moments that are so immediate that audiences come into a personal experience," Huston commented at the time he announced his projected film of *Across the River.* "In that way people no longer are an audience; they become protagonists. Hemingway did this in literature."

Hemingway's story of a venerable army colonel who revisits the European battlegrounds where he fought as a youth, and goes duck hunting one last time before he dies, appealed to Huston very much. As Stuart Kaminsky explains in his book on the writer-director, "Hemingway's novel, like Huston's films, is a search for values by a man of the past, a man who remembers the thrill of battle, male friendships, and hunting; and bravely faces his own death."[10] But Huston has never been able to secure financing for the production, and so the project has remained on the back burner.

Though there are no adaptations of Hemingway's fiction coming out of Hollywood at the moment, TV is once more turning to his short fiction, which can be comfortably dramatized in a one-hour time slot without the need to extend the plot line to the degree that is called for by a feature-length motion picture. In 1977 Public Television telecast a creditable version of "Soldier's Home," which presented Hemingway's story of a veteran's unhappy homecoming in a moving and convincing forty-five-minute teleplay.

Robert Geller, who scripted the teleplay, said in the short interview that followed the telecast that he found dramatizing this story to be challenging because it contains "only one scene of dialogue; the rest is narrative summary. Therefore I tried to flesh out the characters, who exist in the story only in the hero's head as he thinks about them, by presenting them directly in the teleplay in order to show that when the hero leaves home for good at the end he has valid reasons for doing so." So Hemingway continues to be a welcome challenge to those who would adapt his work to a visual medium, a phenomenon that is also illustrated by the superior 1979 teleplay of "My Old Man," which is discussed elsewhere.

Furthermore, it looks like Hemingway's name will continue to light up marquees in a way that he could not have predicted. Two of his granddaughters, Margaux and Mariel, have appeared in films. Mariel in particular seems to have a genuine future in films, having received an Oscar nomination for her role in Woody Allen's *Manhattan* (1979); and to my mind the facial features of Ernest Hemingway unmistakably shine through her face as she appears on the screen.

In looking back on the Hemingway motion pictures discussed in this book, one must concede that none of them is pure Hemingway, and that even the best of them is not flawless. Edward Murray may even be right in his contention that Hemingway's carefully compressed, evocative prose works resist being converted into "screen masterpieces."[11]

Nevertheless, many of the films of Hemingway's fiction have proved to be rewarding cinematic experiences, and some represent excellent examples of the art of adapting a fictional work to the screen. *Islands in the Stream*, for example, is a gem of compression whose screenplay successfully distilled the key elements of Hemingway's diffuse novel. At the other end of the spectrum, where expansion was called for, even Hemingway admitted that Siodmak's *Killers* was an outstanding instance of expansion, since the screenplay extended his short story without diluting the tough-minded intent of its source.

Preserving the spirit of Hemingway's fictional works on film with taste and discrimination calls for gifted screenwriters and directors, and the Hemingway films have attracted some of the best: from scriptwriters like William Faulkner and John Huston to directors like Howard Hawks and Henry King. In addition, some actors have done the best work of their careers in Hemingway-based films; and this is particularly true of Ava Gardner's performances in the 1946 version of *The Killers*, *The Snows of Kilimanjaro*, and *The Sun Also Rises*, each of which is a milestone in her film career. Another case in point is Errol Flynn, whose work in *The Sun Also Rises* marked the peak of his career as a serious actor.

The best of these films, such as *To Have and Have Not, For Whom the Bell Tolls, The Macomber Affair,* and the other films just mentioned above, are very memorable motion pictures indeed. Yet Hemingway thought that the movies of his work would be quickly forgotten, and quoted author Cyril Connolly to this effect in an essay which he wrote in the wake of his own personal involvement with the shooting of *The Old Man and the Sea.* All excursions into "writing for films, however grandiose, are doomed to disappointment," Connolly had said. "It is the nature of such work not to last, so it should never be undertaken" by a serious writer.[12] Yet the continued availability of the Hemingway films on television and in 16mm circulation seems to guarantee that they will last as long as anything he has written. Indeed, the best of these films are an enduring tribute to his achievement as a writer.

"They can't yank a novelist like they can a pitcher," Hemingway once said. "A novelist has to go the full nine. Even if it kills him."[13]

As a writer Ernest Hemingway went the full nine.

Notes*

Chapter 1

¹David Lodge, "Graham Greene," p.937.

²Morris Beja, *Film and Literature*, p.27.

³Robert Nathan, "A Novelist Looks at the Cinema" in *Film: A Montage of Theories*, ed. Richard Dyer McCann, (New York: Dutton, 1966), p.130.

⁴George Bluestone, *Novels into Film*, pp.62–63.

⁵Peter Walsh, *"The Sun Also Rises,"* in *A Library of Film Criticism: American Film Directors*, ed. Stanley Hochman, (New York: Ungar, 1974), p.227.

⁶Ernest Hemingway, *Death in the Afternoon*, p.192.

⁷Edward Murray, *The Cinematic Imagination*, pp.239–40.

⁸Maurice Yacowar, *Tennessee Williams and Film*, p.7.

⁹Jerry Wald, "Screen Adaptation," pp.64–65.

¹⁰John Clark Pratt, "Sometimes a Great Notion: Ernest Hemingway's Roman Catholicism," in *Hemingway in Our*

Full bibliographical information is given only for works not listed in the Selected Bibliography.

(164) **NOTES**

Time, ed. Richard Astro and Jackson Benson, pp. 149–50.

[11]Scott Donaldson, *By Force of Will*, p.75.

[12]Philip Young, *Ernest Hemingway*, p.55.

[13]Ernest Hemingway, "The Christmas Gift," in *By-Line: Ernest Hemingway*, ed. William White, p.404.

[14]Richard Corliss, *Talking Pictures*, p.xxi.

[15]Bernard Dick, "*Graham Greene: The Films of His Fiction*," *Style* 9 (Fall 1975): 560.

[16]Wald, "Screen Adaptation," p.62.

Chapter 2

[1]Carlos Baker, *Ernest Hemingway*, p.54.

[2]Scott Donaldson, *By Force of Will*, p.203.

[3]Ernest Hemingway, *A Farewell to Arms*, p.178.

[4]Arthur Waldhorn, *A Reader's Guide to Ernest Hemingway*, p.130.

[5]Robert Penn Warren, "Ernest Hemingway," in *Ernest Hemingway*, ed. Linda Wagner, p.99.

[6]Ernest Hemingway, *Death in the Afternoon*, p.122.

[7]Charles Higham and Joel Greenberg, *The Celluloid Muse*, p.211.

[8]Frank Borzage, "Directing a Talking Picture," in *Hollywood Directors: 1914–40*, ed. Richard Koszarski, p.235.

[9]David O. Selznick, *Memo From David O. Selznick*, pp.492–505, passim.

[10]Philip Roth, "Another Shy at Hemingway," p.22.

[11]A.E. Hotchner, *Papa Hemingway*, pp.240, 33.

[12]Selznick, *Memo From*, p.489.

Chapter 3

[1]F. Scott Fitzgerald, *The Letters*, pp.300–301.

[2]Otis Ferguson, *The Film Criticism*, p.191.

[3]Anthony Burgess, *Ernest Hemingway and His World*, p.77.

[4]Carlos Baker, *Ernest Hemingway*, p.425.

[5]Linda Wagner, "The Marinating of *For Whom the Bell Tolls*," in *Ernest Hemingway*, ed. Linda Wagner, p.205.

[6]Ernest Hemingway, *For Whom the Bell Tolls*, p.244.

[7]Hemingway, *For Whom*, p.463.

[8]Hemingway, *For Whom*, p.471.

[9]David O. Selznick, *Memo From*, p.377.

[10]Tony Thomas, "Sam Wood," in *The Hollywood Professionals*, vol. 2, ed. Peter Cowie, p.165.

[11]Baker, *Hemingway*, p.471.

[12]"For Whom?" *Time*, 2 August 1943, p.60.

[13]Claude-Edmonde Magny, *The Age of the American Novel*, p.155.

[14]Mary Hemingway, Letter to Gene Phillips.

Chapter 4

[1]Ernest Hemingway, *To Have and Have Not*, p.225.

[2]William Faulkner, *Selected Letters*, p.180.

[3]James Meriwether and Michael Millgate, eds., *Lion in the Garden*, p.241.

[4]Frank Laurence, "The Film Adaptations of Hemingway: Hollywood and the Hemingway Myth" (Ph.D. diss., University of Pennsylvania, 1970), p.232.

[5]Richard Lillich, "Hemingway on the Screen," p. 213.

[6]Laurence, "Film Adaptations," p.220.

[7]Milt Machlin, *The Private Hell of Ernest Hemingway*, p.209.

[8]Stuart Kaminsky, *Don Siegel*, p.131.

Chapter 5

[1]Colin McArthur, *Underworld USA*, p.105.

[2]Philip Young, "Big World Out There: The Nick Adams

Stories" in *The Short Stories of Ernest Hemingway*, ed. Jackson Benson, p.35.

[3]Robert Siodmak, "Hoodlums: The Myth" in *Hollywood Directors: 1941–76*, ed. Richard Koszarski, p.286.

[4]Mary Hemingway, Letter to Gene Phillips.

[5]A. E. Hotchner, *Papa Hemingway*, p.107.

[6]Stuart Kaminsky, *Don Siegel*, p.176.

[7]A.E. Hotchner, "One Thing After Another," p.86.

[8]Pauline Kael, *I Lost It at the Movies*, p.201.

[9]Philip Young, *Ernest Hemingway*, p.55.

[10]Hotchner, "One Thing After Another," p.86.

[11]Carlos Baker, *Ernest Hemingway*, p.589.

[12]"A Very Short Story" is not included in Philip Young's collection of the Nick Adams stories first published in 1972, but there seems to be no reason to except it. It is true that Nick is not specifically named as the hero of the tale, but neither is his name mentioned in some of the other stories included in Young's anthology. Suffice it to say here that the story fits perfectly into the set of Nick Adams stories and was placed by Hemingway in the volume of short stories called *In Our Time* right after the brief episode describing Nick's being wounded in battle.

[13]Ernest Hemingway, *For Whom the Bell Tolls*, p.339.

[14]Hotchner, "One Thing After Another," p.89.

[15]Herb Lightman, "Two-Continent Assignment," p.631.

[16]Ernest Hemingway, "The Battler," in *The Nick Adams Stories*, p.37.

Chapter 6

[1]A.E. Hotchner, "One Thing After Another," pp.72, 76.

[2]Richard Corliss, *Talking Pictures*, p.263.

[3]Carlos Baker, *Ernest Hemingway*, p.363.

[4]Scott Donaldson, *By Force of Will*, p.171.

[5]Ernest Hemingway, "Notes on Dangerous Game," in *By-Line: Ernest Hemingway*, p.144.

[6]Joel Greenberg, "Writing for the Movies," p.10.

[7]Arthur Waldhorn, *A Reader's Guide to Ernest Hemingway*, p.149.

[8]Charles Higham, *Hollywood Cameramen*, pp.131–32.

[9]Robert Morsberger, "That Hemingway Kind of Love," p.55.

[10]A. E. Hotchner, *Papa Hemingway*, p.109.

[11]Greenberg, "Writing for the Movies," p.17.

[12]Ernest Hemingway, "On Writing," in *The Nick Adams Stories*, p.217.

[13]Ernest Hemingway, "My Old Man," in *In Our Time*, pp.118, 129.

[14]George Morris, *John Garfield*, p.135.

[15]Baker, *Ernest Hemingway*, p.895.

Chapter 7

[1]Ernest Hemingway, "The Snows of Kilimanjaro," in *The Snows of Killimanjaro and Other Stories*, p.11.

[2]Ernest Hemingway, *Green Hills of Africa*, p.17.

[3]Casey Robinson, "Adaptor's Views," p.4.

[4]Anthony Burgess, *Ernest Hemingway and His World*, p.68.

[5]Carlos Baker, *Ernest Hemingway*, p.643.

[6]Charles Higham, *Hollywood Cameramen*, p.31.

[7]Judith M. Kass, *Ava Gardner*, pp.66, 69.

[8]Lionel Godfrey, "It Wasn't Like That in the Book," p.14.

[9]Kass, *Ava*, p.68.

[10]George Plimpton, "An Interview with Ernest Hemingway," in *Ernest Hemingway*, ed. Linda Wagner, p.31.

[11]Baker, *Hemingway*, p.231.

[12]Ernest Hemingway, *Death in the Afternoon*, p.91.

[13]Ernest Hemingway, *The Sun Also Rises*, p.243.

[14]Ernest Hemingway, *A Moveable Feast*, p.29.

[15]Arthur Waldhorn, *A Reader's Guide to Ernest Hemingway*, p.106.

[16]Joseph McBride and Gerald Peary, "Hawks Talks," p.50.

[17]A.E. Hotchner, *Papa Hemingway*, p.201.

[18]Arthur Knight, "Hemingway into Film," p.33.

[19]Edward Murray, *The Cinematic Imagination*, p.236.

[20]Roy Pickard, "The Tough Race," p.44.

[21]Godfrey, "It Wasn't Like That," p.14.

[22]Hotchner, *Papa*, p.33.

[23]Mike Steen, *A Look at Tennessee Williams*, p.189.

Chapter 8

[1]Ernest Hemingway, "On the Blue Water: A Gulf Stream Letter," in *By-Line: Ernest Hemingway*, p.208.

[2]Ernest Hemingway, *A Farewell to Arms*, p.178.

[3]Ernest Hemingway, *The Old Man and the Sea*, p.103.

[4]Carlos Baker, *Ernest Hemingway*, pp.639, 670, 676.

[5]Baker, *Hemingway*, p.643.

[6]Mary Hemingway, Letter to Gene Phillips.

[7]Ernest Hemingway, "A Situation Report," in *By-Line: Ernest Hemingway*, p.415.

[8]Mary Hemingway, Letter.

[9]Fred Zinnemann, Letter to Gene Phillips.

[10]Gordon Gow, "The Fifties," in *Hollywood: 1920–1970*, ed. Peter Cowie, p.186.

[11]Leicester Hemingway, *My Brother, Ernest Hemingway*, p.276.

[12]Scott Donaldson, *By Force of Will*, p.249.

[13]Ernest Hemingway, "A Situation Report," p.413.

[14]Larry Swindell, *Spencer Tracy*, p.208.

[15]Gow, "The Fifties," p.186.

[16]"Two with Tracy," p.42.

[17]Gow, "The Fifties," p.186.

[18]A.E. Hotchner, *Papa Hemingway*, p.33.

[19]Peter Bart, "*Islands*," p.22.

[20]Frank Laurence, "The Film Adaptations of Hemingway," p.37.

[21]Bart, "*Islands*," p.22.

[22]Bart, "*Islands*," p.22.

[23]Brendan Gill, "Novels into Films," p.45.

[24]Christopher Porterfield, "The Big One Gets Away Again," p.89.

[25]Cf. Ernest Hemingway, *For Whom the Bell Tolls*, p.467.

[26]Cf. Ernest Hemingway, *Islands in the Stream*, p.435.

Chapter 9

[1]"The Hero of the Code," p.87.

[2]Carlos Baker, *Ernest Hemingway*, p.72.

[3]Anthony Burgess, *Ernest Hemingway and His World*, p.53.

[4]John Clark Pratt, "Ernest Hemingway's Roman Catholicism," in *Hemingway in Our Time*, ed. Richard Astro and Jackson Benson, p.147.

[5]Baker, *Ernest*, pp.239; 688.

[6]A.E. Hotchner, *Papa Hemingway*, p.142.

[7]Baker, *Hemingway*, p.672.

[8]Ernest Hemingway, "The Big Two-Hearted River," in *The Nick Adams Stories*, pp.160–61, 165.

[9]Hotchner, *Papa*, pp.108, 222.

[10]Stuart Kaminsky, *John Huston*, p.203.

[11]Edward Murray, *The Cinematic Imagination*, p.243.

[12]Ernest Hemingway, "A Situation Report," in *By-Line: Ernest Hemingway*, p.413.

[13]Lillian Ross, "How Do You Like It Now, Gentlemen?" in *Hemingway*, ed. Robert P. Weeks, p.18.

Film Rental Sources

A Farewell to Arms (1932)	CFM
A Farewell to Arms (1957)	FI
For Whom the Bell Tolls	TWY, UNI
Hemingway's Adventures of a Young Man	FI
Islands in the Stream	P
The Killers (1946)	UNI
The Killers (1964)	UNI
The Old Man and the Sea	AB, TWY
The Spanish Earth	AB
The Sun Also Rises	FI
To Have and Have Not	UA

AB
Audio Brandon Films
(Macmillan)
34 MacQuesten Parkway
South

Mount Vernon, New York
10550
(914) 664–5051
or

(170)

1619 North Cherokee
Los Angeles, California
   90028
(213) 463–0357
   or
Branch offices in Oakland,
Dallas, and Brookfield,
   Illinois

CFM
Classic Film Museum
Dover-Foxcraft, Maine
   04426

FI
Films Incorporated
4420 Oakton Street
Skokie, Illinois 60076
(312) 676–1088
   or
440 Park Avenue South
New York, New York 10016
(212) 889–7910
   or
5625 Hollywood Boulevard
Hollywood, California
   90028
(213) 466–5481
   or
Branch offices in Atlanta,
Boston,
Salt Lake City,
and San Diego

P
Paramount 16
5454 Marathon Street
Hollywood, California
   90038
(213) 462–0700

TWY
Twyman Films
321 Salem Avenue
Dayton, Ohio 45401
(513) 222–4014

UA
United Artists Sixteen
729 Seventh Avenue
New York, New York 10019
(212) 575–3000

UNI
Universal Sixteen
445 Park Avenue
New York, New York 10022
(212) 759–7500
   or
8901 Beverly Blvd
Los Angeles, California
90048
(213) 550–7461
   or
Branch offices in Atlanta,
Chicago, and Dallas

Filmography

A Farewell to Arms (1932). *Director/Producer:* Frank Borzage. *Screenwriters:* Benjamin Glazer *and* Oliver H. P. Garrett. *Photography:* Charles Lang. *Art Directors:* Roland Anderson *and* Hans Drier. *Editor:* Otho Lovering. Paramount. 78 minutes.

> *Frederic Henry* (Gary Cooper). *Catherine Barkley* (Helen Hayes). *Rinaldi* (Adolphe Menjou). *Helen Ferguson* (Mary Phillips). *Priest* (Jack LaRue). *Head nurse* (Blanche Frederici). *Bonello* (Henry Armetta). *Piani* (George Humbert). *Manera* (Fred Malatesta). *Miss Van Campen* (Mary Forbes). *Count Greffi* (Tom Ricketts). *Gordoni* (Robert Cauterio). *British major* (Gilbert Emery).

The Spanish Earth (1937). *Director/Producer:* Joris Ivens. *Scenario:* Archibald MacLeish *and* Lillian Hellman. *Photography:* Joris Ivens *and* John Ferno. *Music compiled by* Virgil Thompson *and* Marc Blitzstein. *Commentary written and spoken by* Ernest Hemingway. Contemporary Historians. 54 minutes.

For Whom the Bell Tolls (1943). *Director/Producer:* Sam Wood. *Screenwriter:* Dudley Nichols. *Photographer:* Ray Rennahan. *Production Designer:* William Cameron Menzies. *Art Directors:* Hans Drier *and* Haldane Douglas. *Music:* Victor Young. *Editors:* Sherman Todd *and* John Link. Paramount. 168 minutes, cut to 134 minutes.

   Robert Jordan (Gary Cooper). *Maria* (Ingrid Bergman). *Pilar* (Katina Paxinou). *Pablo* (Akim Tamiroff). *Agustin* (Arturo de Cordova). *Anselmo* (Vladimir Sokoloff). *Rafael* (Mikhail Rasumny). *Fernando* (Fortunio Bonanova). *Andres* (Eric Feldary). *Primitivo* (Victor Varconi). *El Sordo* (Joseph Calleia). *Joaquin* (Lilo Yarson). *Paco* (Alexander Granach). *Gustavo* (Adia Kuznetzoff). *Ignacio* (Leonid Snegoff). *Andre Massart* (George Coulouris). *General Golz* (Leo Bulgakov). *Lieutenant Berrendo* (Duncan Renaldo). *Captain Gomez* (Frank Puglia). *Colonel Miranda* (Pedro de Cordoba). *Staff Officer* (Michael Visaroff). *Karkov* (Konstantin Shayne). *Captain Mora* (Martin Garralaga). *Colonel Duval* (Jack Mylong). *Sniper* (Jean Del Val). *Kashkin* (Feodor Chaliapin). *Don Guillermo* (Antonio Vidal). *Don Guillermo's wife* (Soledad Jiminez). *Don Ricardo* (Mayo Newhall). *Don Benito Garcia* (Michael Dalmatoff). *Don Faustino Rivero* (Robert Tafur). *Julian* (Armand Roland). *Drunk* (Luis Rojas). *Singer* (Trini Varela). *Sergeant* (Dick Botiller). *Cavalry man* (Yakima Canutt). *First sentry* (Tito Renaldo). *Girl in café* (Yvonne de Carlo).

To Have and Have Not (1944). *Director/Producer:* Howard Hawks. *Screenwriters:* Jules Furthman *and* William Faulkner. *Photographer:* Sidney Hickox. *Art Director:* Charles Novi. *Music:* Leo Forbstein. *Editor:* Christian Nyby. Warner Brothers. 100 minutes.

   Harry Morgan (Humphrey Bogart). *Eddie* (Walter Brennan). *Marie Browning* (Lauren Bacall). *Cricket* (Hoagy Carmichael). *Hellene de Bursac* (Dolores Moran). *Paul de Bursac* (Walter Molnar). *Lieutenant Coyo* (Sheldon Leonard). *Gerard* (Marcel Dalio). *Johnson* (Walter Sande).

Captain Renard (Dan Seymour). *Beauclerc* (Paul Marion). *Mrs. Beauclerc* (Patricia Shay). *Rosalie* (Janette Grae). *Horatio* (Sir Lancelot). *Emil* (Emmett Smith). *Bodyguard* (Aldo Nadi). *Bartender* (Pat West). *Quartermaster* (Eugene Borden). *Civilian* (Pedro Regas). *Headwaiter* (Major Fred Farrell). *Cashiers* (Adrienne d'Ambricourt. Marguerita Sylva). *Chef* (Joseph Milani). *Detective* (Hal Kelly). *Dancer* (Audrey Armstrong). *Naval ensign* (Ron Randell). *Gaullists* (Fred Dosch. Maurice Marsao. Louis Mercier. George Suzanne. Crane Whitley). *Urchins* (Elzie Emanuel. Harold Garrison).

The Killers (1946). *Director:* Robert Siodmak. *Producer:* Mark Hellinger. *Screenwriters:* Anthony Veiller *and* John Huston (uncredited). *Photographer:* Woody Bredell. *Art Directors:* Jack Otterson *and* Martin Obzina. *Music:* Miklos Rosza. *Editor:* Arthur Hilton. Universal. 105 minutes.

Swede (Burt Lancaster). *Kitty Collins* (Ava Gardner). *Jim Reardon* (Edmond O'Brien). *Big Jim Colfax* (Albert Dekker). *Sam Lubinsky* (Sam Levene). *Al* (Charles McGraw). *Max* (William Conrad). *Nick Adams* (Phil Brown). *Mrs. Hirsch* (Vera Lewis). *George* (Harry Hayden). *Queenie* (Queenie Smith). *Joe* (Garry Owen). *Kenyon* (Donald MacBride). *Jake* (John Miljan). *Lilly* (Virginia Christine). *Charleston* (Vince Barnett). *Packy Robinson* (Charles D. Brown). *Sam* (Bill Walker). *Dum Dum* (Jack Lambert). *Blinky* (Jeff Corey). *Charlie* (Wally Scott). *Ginny* (Gabrielle Windsor). *Plunther* (John Berkes). *Farmer Brown* (Charles Middleton). *Lou Tingle* (Noel Cravat). *Stella* (Ann Staunton). *Gimp* (Ernie Adams). *Pete* (Michael Hale). *Paymaster* (Harry Brown). *Assistant paymaster* (Audley Anderson). *Timekeeper* (Mike Donovan). *Customer* (Al Hill). *Bartender* (Wally Rose). *Minister* (Rev. Neal Dodd). *Motorman* (William Ruhl). *Conductor* (Ethan Laidlaw). *Housekeeper* (Therese Lyon). *Nurse* (Beatrice Roberts). *Doctors* (John Sheehan. George Anderson). *Police chief* (Howard Freeman). *Police driver* (Jack Cheatham). *Policemen* (Howard

Neglev. Perc Launders. Geoffrey Ingham). *Waiters* (Milton Wallace. Nolan Leary. John Trebach). *Man* (Rex Dale).

The Macomber Affair (1947). Based on "The Short Happy Life of Francis Macomber." *Director:* Zoltan Korda. *Producers:* Benedict Bogeaus *and* Casey Robinson. *Screenwriters:* Casey Robinson *and* Seymour Bennett. *Photographer:* Karl Struss. *Art Director:* Erno Metzner. *Editors:* George Feld *and* Jack Wheeler. *Music:* Miklos Rosza. United Artists. 89 minutes.

 Francis Macomber (Robert Preston). *Margaret Macomber* (Joan Bennett). *Robert Wilson* (Gregory Peck). *Police inspector* (Reginald Denny). *Kongoni* (Earl Smith). *Aimee* (Jean Gillie). *Coroner* (Carl Harbord).

Under My Skin. Based on "My Old Man." (1950). *Director:* Jean Negulesco. *Screenwriter/Producer:* Casey Robinson. *Photographer:* Joseph La Shelle. *Art Directors:* Lyle Wheeler *and* Maurice Ranstord. *Editor:* Dorothy Spencer. *Music:* Danille Amfitheatrof. Twentieth Century-Fox. 86 minutes.

 Dan Butler (John Garfield). *Joe* (Orley Lindgren). *Paule Manet* (Micheline Preslle). *Louis Bork* (Luther Adler). *George Gardner* (Noel Drayton). *Maurice* (A. A. Merola). *Rico* (Ott George). *Max* (Paul Bryar). *Henriette* (Ann Codee). *Bartender* (Steve Geray).

The Breaking Point (1950). Based on *To Have and Have Not.* *Director:* Michael Curtiz. *Producer:* Jerry Wald. *Screenwriter:* Ranald MacDougall. *Photographer:* Ted McCord. *Art Director:* Edward Carrere. *Editor:* Alan Crosland, Jr. *Music:* Ray Heindorf. Warner Brothers. 94 minutes.

 Harry Morgan (John Garfield). *Leona Charles* (Patricia Neal). *Lucy Morgan* (Phyllis Thaxter). *Wesley Park* (Juano Hernandez). *Duncan* (Wallace Ford). *Rogers* (Edmon Ryan). *Hannagan* (Ralph Dumke). *Danny* (Guy Thomajan). *Concho* (William Campbell). *Amelia* (Sherry Jackson). *Connie* (Donna Jo Boyce). *Mr. Sing* (Victor Sen

Yung). *Macho* (Peter Brocco). *Gotch* (John Doucette). *Charlie* (James Griffith).

The Snows of Kilimanjaro (1952). *Director:* Henry King. *Producers:* Darryl F. Zanuck *and* Casey Robinson (uncredited). *Screenwriter:* Casey Robinson. *Photographer:* Leon Shamroy. *Art Directors:* Lyle Wheeler *and* John De Cuir. *Editor:* Barbara McLean. *Music:* Bernard Herrmann. Twentieth Century-Fox. 114 minutes.

Harry (Gregory Peck). *Helen* (Susan Hayward). *Cynthia* (Ava Gardner). *Countess Liz* (Hildegarde Neff). *Uncle Bill* (Leo G. Carroll). *Johnson* (Torin Thatcher). *Beatrice* (Ava Norring). *Connie* (Helen Stanley). *Emile* (Marcel Dalio). *Guitarist* (Vincent Gomez). *Spanish dancer* (Richard Allan). *Dr. Simmons* (Leonard Carey). *Witch doctor* (Paul Thompson). *Molo* (Emmett Smith). *Charles* (Victor Wood). *American soldier* (Bert Freed). *Margot* (Agnes Laury). *Georgette* (Monique Chantel). *Annette* (Janine Grandel). *Compton* (John Dodsworth). *Young Harry* (Charles Bates). *Venduse* (Lisa Ferraday). *Princess* (Maya Van Horn). *Marquis* (Ivan Lebedeff). *Spanish officer* (Martin Garralaga). *Servant* (George Davis). *Old waiter* (Julian Rivero). *Clerk* (Edward Colmans). *Accordian players* (Ernest Brunner. Arthur Brunner).

The Sun Also Rises (1957). *Director:* Henry King. *Producer:* Darryl F. Zanuck. *Screenwriter:* Peter Viertel. *Photographer:* Leo Tover. *Art Directors:* Lyle Wheeler *and* Mark-Lee Kirk. *Editor:* William Mace. *Music:* Hugo Friedhofer *and* Alexander Courage. *Bullfight Director:* Miguel Delgado. Twentieth Century-Fox. 129 minutes.

Jake Barnes (Tyrone Power). *Brett Ashley* (Ava Gardner). *Robert Cohn* (Mel Ferrer). *Mike Campbell* (Errol Flynn). *Bill Gorton* (Eddie Albert). *Pedro Romero* (Robert Evans). *Count Mippipopolous* (Gregory Ratoff). *Harris* (Bob Cunningham). *Frances Cohn* (Rebecca Iturbi). *Braddock* (Eduardo Noreiga). *Mrs. Braddock* (Jacqueline Evans).

Montoya (Carlos Muzquiz). *Georgette* (Juliette Greco). *Zizi* (Marcel Dalio). *Doctor* (Henry Daniell). *Girl* (Danik Patisson). *English girl* (Lilia Guizar). *Romero's manager* (Carlos David Ortigos). *American at bullfight* (Lee Morgan).

A Farewell to Arms (1957). *Director:* Charles Vidor. *Producer:* David O. Selznick. *Screenwriter:* Ben Hecht. *Photographers:* Pietro Portalupi *and* Oswald Morris. *Art Directors:* Alfred Junge *and* Mario Garbuglia. *Editors:* James E. Newman, Gerald J. Wilson, *and* John M. Foley. *Music:* Mario Nascimbene. Twentieth Century-Fox. 152 minutes.

Frederic Henry (Rock Hudson). *Catherine Barkley* (Jennifer Jones). *Rinaldi* (Vittorio de Sica). *Helen Ferguson* (Elaine Stritch). *Father Galli* (Alberto Sordi). *Miss Van Campen* (Mercedes McCambridge). *Dr. Emerich* (Oscar Homolka). *Bonello* (Kurt Kaszner). *Passini* (Leopoldo Trieste). *Aymo* (Franco Interlenghi). *Major Stampi* (Jose Nieto). *Captain Bassi* (Georges Brehat). *Colonel Valentini* (Victor Francen). *Nino* (Memmo Carotenuto). *Nurse* (Joan Shawlee).

The Gun Runners (1958). Based on *To Have and Have Not*. *Director:* Don Siegel. *Producer:* Clarence Greene. *Screenwriters:* Daniel Mainwaring *and* Paul Monash. *Photographer:* Hal Mohr. *Art Director:* Howard Richmond. *Editor:* Chester Schaeffer. *Music:* Leith Stevens. United Artists. 83 minutes.

Sam Martin (Audie Murphy). *Hanagan* (Eddie Albert). *Lucy Martin* (Patricia Owens). *Harvey* (Everett Sloane). *Eva* (Gita Hall). *Buzurski* (Richard Jaeckel). *Arnold* (Jack Elam). *Sy Phillips* (Paul Birch). *Peterson* (John Harding). *Pop* (John Qualen). *Blonde* (Peggy Maley). *Carlos* (Carlos Romero). *Juan* (Edward Colmans). *Pepita* (Lita Leon). *Pepito* (Steven Peck). *Commander Walsh* (Ted Jacques). *Berenguer* (Freddie Roberto).

The Old Man and the Sea (1958). *Director:* John Sturges. *Producer:* Leland Hayward. *Screenwriter:* Peter Viertel. *Photog-*

rapher: James Wong Howe. *Art Directors:* Art Loeland *and* Edward Carrere. *Music:* Dimitri Tiomkin. Warner Brothers. 87 minutes.

> *Old Man* (Spencer Tracy). *Boy* (Felipe Pazos). *Martin* (Harry Bellaver). *Café proprietor* (Don Diamond). *Hand wrestler* (Don Blackman). *Professional gambler* (Joey Ray). *Other gamblers* (Richard Alameda. Robert Alderette. Mauritz Hugo. Carlos Rivera. Tony Rosa. Ernest Hemingway). *Tourist* (Mary Hemingway).

Hemingway's Adventures of a Young Man (1962). Based on *The Nick Adams Stories. Director:* Martin Ritt. *Producer:* Jerry Wald. *Screenwriter:* A. E. Hotchner. *Photographer:* Lee Garmes. *Art Directors:* John Martin Smith *and* Paul Groesse. *Editor:* Hugh S. Fowler. *Music:* Franz Waxman. Twentieth Century-Fox. 145 minutes.

> *Nick Adams* (Richard Beymer). *Dr. Adams* (Arthur Kennedy). *Mrs. Adams* (Jessica Tandy). *George* (Michael J. Pollard). *Joe Bolton* (Simon Oakland). *Eddy Bolton* (Marc Cavell). *Billy Tabeshaw* (Pat Hogan). *The Battler* (Paul Newman). *Bugs* (Juano Hernandez). *Brakeman* (Edward Binns). *Carolyn* (Diane Baker). *Contessa* (Corinne Calvert). *Rosanna* (Susan Strasberg). *Major Padula* (Ricardo Montalban). *Turner* (Fred Clark). *Billy Campbell* (Dan Dailey). *Telegrapher* (James Dunn). *John* (Eli Wallach). *Ludstrom* (Whit Bissell). *Mayor* (Charles Fredericks). *Montecito* (Philip Bourneuf). *Greffi* (Tullio Carminati).

The Killers (1964). *Director/Producer:* Don Siegel. *Screenwriter:* Gene L. Coon. *Photographer:* Richard L. Rawlings. *Art Directors:* Frank Arrigo *and* George Chan. *Editor:* Richard Belding. *Music:* Johnny Williams. Universal-International. 95 minutes.

> *Charlie* (Lee Marvin). *Sheila Farr* (Angie Dickinson). *Johnny North* (John Cassavetes). *Browning* (Ronald Reagan). *Lee* (Clu Gulager). *Earl Sylvester* (Claude Akins). *Mickey* (Norman Fell). *Miss Watson* (Virginia Christine).

George (Robert Phillips). *Desk clerk* (Seymour Cassel). *Receptionist* (Kathleen O'Malley). *Salesman* (Jimmy Joyce). *Gym assistant* (Ted Jacques). *Mail truck driver* (Don Haggerty). *Mail truck guard* (Irvin Mosley).

Islands in the Stream (1977). *Director:* Franklin J. Schaffner. *Producers:* Peter Bart *and* Max Palevsky. *Screenwriter:* Denne Bart Petitclerc. *Photographer:* Fred J. Koenekamp. *Art Director:* William J. Creber. *Editor:* Robert Swink. *Music:* Jerry Goldsmith. Paramount. 105 minutes.

Thomas Hudson (George C. Scott). *Audrey* (Claire Bloom). *Eddy* (David Hemmings). *Captain Ralph* (Gilbert Roland). *Lil* (Susan Tyrrell). *Joseph* (Julius Harris). *Willy* (Richard Evans). *Tommy* (Hart Bochner). *David* (Michael Wixted). *Andrew* (Brad Savage).

Selected
Bibliography

Works by Ernest Hemingway

(The original date of publication appears after the title when
the edition consulted is of a later date.)

In Our Time (1925). New York: Scribner's, 1958.

The Sun Also Rises (1926). New York: Scribner's, 1954.

Men Without Women (1927). New York: Scribner's, 1955.

A Farewell to Arms (1929). New York: Scribner's, 1957.

Death in the Afternoon (1932). New York: Scribner's, 1960.

Green Hills of Africa (1935). New York: Scribner's, 1963.

To Have and Have Not (1937). New York: Scribner's, 1962.

The Snows of Kilimanjaro and Other Stories (1938). New York:
Scribner's, 1964.

The Spanish Earth. Cleveland: Savage, 1938.

For Whom the Bell Tolls (1940). New York: Scribner's, 1968.

The Old Man and the Sea. New York: Scribner's, 1952.

"A Tribute to Mamma" [sic] (1952). In *Authors on Film*. Edited
by Harry M. Geduld, pp.283–84. Bloomington: Indiana
University Press, 1972. A tribute to Marlene Dietrich.

A Moveable Feast (1964). New York: Bantam Books, 1970.

By-Line: Ernest Hemingway: Selected Articles and Dispatches of Four Decades (1967), Edited by William White. New York: Bantam Books, 1968.

The Fifth Column and Four Stories of the Spanish Civil War (1969). New York: Bantam Books, 1970.

Islands in the Stream (1970). New York: Bantam Books, 1972.

The Nick Adams Stories (1972). Edited by Philip Young. New York: Bantam Books, 1973.

Works about Ernest Hemingway

Astro, Richard, and Jackson Benson, eds. *Hemingway: In Our Time*. Corvallis: Oregon State University Press, 1974.

Baker, Carlos. *Ernest Hemingway: A Life Story*. New York: Bantam Books, 1970.

Bart, Peter. "*Islands:* A Film with Hemingway in Mind." *The Los Angeles Times Calendar*, 13 March 1977, p.22.

Beja, Morris. *Film and Literature*. New York: Longman, 1979.

Benson, Jackson, ed. *The Short Stories of Ernest Hemingway: Critical Essays*. Durham: Duke University Press, 1975.

Bluestone, George. *Novels into Film*. Berkeley: University of California Press, 1957.

Burgess, Anthony. *Ernest Hemingway and His World*. New York: Scribner's, 1978.

Corliss, Richard. *Talking Pictures: Screenwriters in the American Cinema*. New York: Penguin Books, 1975.

Cowie, Peter, ed. *Hollywood: 1920–1970*. New York: Barnes, 1977.

————, ed. *The Hollywood Professionals*. 3 vols. New York: Barnes, 1973–74.

Dick, Bernard. "Graham Greene." Style, 9 (Fall 1975): 558–60.

Donaldson, Scott. *By Force of Will: The Life and Art of Ernest Hemingway*. New York: Viking, 1977.

Ferguson, Otis. *The Film Criticism*. Edited by Robert Wilson. Philadelphia: Temple University Press, 1971.

Faulkner, William. *Selected Letters*. Edited by Joseph Blotner. New York: Random House, 1977.

Fitzgerald, F. Scott. *The Letters*. Edited by Andrew Turnbull. New York: Dell, 1966.

Gill, Brendan. "Novels into Film." *Film Comment* 13 (March-April 1977): 44–45.

Godfrey, Lionel. "It Wasn't Like That in the Book." *Films and Filming*, April 1967, pp.12–16.

Greenberg, Joel. "Writing for the Movies: Casey Robinson." *Focus on Film*, Spring 1979, pp.7–24.

Hemingway, Gregory M. *Papa: A Personal Memoir*. New York: Bantam Books, 1977.

Hemingway, Leicester. *My Brother, Ernest Hemingway*. Cleveland: World, 1962.

Hemingway, Mary. *How It Was*. New York: Knopf, 1976.

"The Hero of the Code." *Time*, 14 July 1961, pp.87–90.

Higham, Charles. *Hollywood Cameramen: Sources of Light*. Bloomington: Indiana University Press, 1970.

———, and Joel Greenberg. *The Celluloid Muse: Hollywood Directors Speak*. New York: New American Library, 1972.

Hochman, Stanley, ed. *A Library of Film Criticism: American Film Directors*. New York: Ungar, 1974.

Hotchner, A.E. "One Thing After Another: The Adaptation." In *The Eighth Art: Twenty-Three Views of Television Today*, pp.71–89. New York: Holt, Rinehart and Winston, 1962.

———. *Papa Hemingway: A Personal Memoir*. New York: Bantam Books, 1967.

"It's Hemingway's Year." *Newsweek*, 16 December 1957, pp.116, 119.

Jordan, René. *Gary Cooper*. New York: Pyramid, 1974.

Kael, Pauline. *I Lost It at the Movies*. New York: Bantam Books, 1966.

Kaminsky, Stuart. *Don Siegel: Director*. New York: Curtis Books, 1974.

————. *Gary Cooper*. New York: St. Martin's, 1979.

————. *John Huston: Maker of Magic*. Boston: Houghton, Mifflin, 1978.

————. "Literary Adaptation and Change: *The Killers*." In *American Film Genres*, pp.62–84. New York: Dell, 1977.

Kass, Judith M. *Ava Gardner*. New York: Harvest Books, 1977.

Kawin, Bruce. *Faulkner and Film*. New York: Ungar, 1977.

————. "Fishing for a Writer." In *To Have and Have Not*. Introduction to the screenplay by Jules Furthman and William Faulkner. Madison: University of Wisconsin Press, 1979.

Knight, Arthur. "Hemingway into Film." *Saturday Review*, 29 July 1961, pp.33–34.

Koszarski, Richard, ed. *Hollywood Directors: 1914–1940*. New York: Oxford University Press, 1976.

————, ed. *Hollywood Directors: 1941–1976*. New York: Oxford University Press, 1977.

Laurence, Frank. "Death in the Matinée: The Film Endings of Hemingway's Fiction." *Literature/Film Quarterly* 2 (Winter 1974):44–51.

Lightman, Herb. "Two-Continent Assignment: Filming *Hemingway's Adventures of a Young Man*." *American Cinematographer*, October 1962, pp.604–605, 631–34.

Lillich, Richard. "Hemingway on the Screen." *Films in Review* 10 (April 1959):208–18.

Lodge, David. "*Graham Greene*." *The Tablet* (London), 28 September 1974, p.937.

Machlin, Milt. *The Private Hell of Ernest Hemingway*. New York: Paperback Library, 1962.

Magny, Claude-Edmonde. *The Age of the American Novel: The Film Aesthetic of Fiction Between the Two Wars*. Translated by Eleanor Hochman. New York: Ungar, 1972.

McArthur, Colin. *Underworld USA*. New York: Viking, 1972.

McBride, Joseph, and Gerald Peary. "Hawks Talks." *Film Comment* 10 (May 1974):pp.44–53.

Meriwether, James, and Michael Millgate, eds. *Lion in the Garden: Interviews with William Faulkner, 1926–1962*. New York: Random House, 1968.

Morris, George. *John Garfield*. New York: Harvest Books, 1977.

Morsberger, Robert. "That Hemingway Kind of Love: 'Macomber' in the Movies." *Literature/Film Quarterly* 4 (Winter, 1976):54–59.

Murray, Edward. *The Cinematic Imagination: Writers and the Motion Pictures*. New York: Ungar, 1972.

Peary, Gerald, and Roger Shatzkin, eds. *The Classic American Novel and the Movies*. New York: Ungar, 1977.

———. *The Modern American Novel and the Movies*. New York: Ungar, 1978.

Pickard, Roy. "The Tough Race: The Films of Henry King." *Films and Filming*, September 1971, pp.38–44.

Porterfield, Christopher. "The Big One Gets Away Again." *Time*, 21 March 1977, p.89.

Robinson, Casey. "Adaptor's Views." *The New York Times*, 12 October 1952, p.4.

Roth, Philip. "Another Shy at Hemingway." *The New Republic*, 12 February 1958, p.22.

Rovit, Earl. *Ernest Hemingway*. New York: Twayne, 1963.

Selznick, David O. *Memo From David O. Selznick*. edited by Rudy Behlmer. New York: Avon Books, 1973.

Shaw, Samuel. *Ernest Hemingway*. New York: Ungar, 1973.

Steen, Mike. *A Look at Tennessee Williams*. New York: Hawthorn Books, 1969.

Stephens, Robert, ed. *Ernest Hemingway: The Critical Reception*. New York: Franklin, 1977.

Swindell, Larry. *Spencer Tracy*. New York: New American Library, 1971.

Thomas, Tony. *Gregory Peck*. New York: Pyramid, 1977.

"Two with Tracy." *Time*, 13 October 1958, p.42.

Wagner, Linda, ed. *Ernest Hemingway: Five Decades of Criticism*. Ann Arbor: Michigan State University Press, 1974.

Wald, Jerry. "Screen Adaptation." *Films in Review* 5 (1954):62–67.

Waldhorn, Arthur. *A Reader's Guide to Ernest Hemingway*. New York: Farrar, Straus & Giroux, 1973.

Weeks, Robert, ed. *Hemingway: A Collection of Critical Essays*. Englewood Cliffs, N.J.: Prentice-Hall, 1962.

Yacowar, Maurice. *Tennessee Williams and Film*. New York: Ungar, 1977.

Young, Philip. *Ernest Hemingway: A Reconsideration*. University Park: Pennsylvania State Press, 1966.

Unpublished Materials

Hemingway, Mary. Letter to Gene Phillips. August 20, 1978.

Laurence, Frank. "The Film Adaptations of Hemingway: Hollywood and the Hemingway Myth." Ph.D. dissertation, University of Pennsylvania, 1970.

Zinnemann, Fred. Letter to Gene Phillips. September 8, 1978.

Index

(187)